ALAN BOLD was born in Edinburgh in 1943. At fifteen he started work as a garage hand, then he became an apprentice baker, but later returned to school. He was educated at Edinburgh University where he was active in student journalism, and as the co-leader and alto-saxophonist in a modern jazz group. After university he worked on the editorial staff of *The Times Educational Supplement*, then freelanced for various newspapers. He has lectured on the relationship of poetry to politics and science, and has often read his poetry on television and throughout the country. He was awarded a Scottish Arts Council grant in 1967. In 1965 his first book, *Society Inebrious*, was published, followed by *The Voyage*, a Baudelaire translation, in 1966, *To Find the New* (1967), and *A Perpetual Motion Machine* (1969). His next book will contain the long poem *The State of the Nation*. He is editor of *The Penguin Book of Socialist Verse*. Alan Bold is married to an art teacher; their daughter, Valentina, is named after the first woman in space.

EDWARD BRATHWAITE was born in Barbados in 1930, and was educated there and at Pembroke College, Cambridge, where he read history. From 1955 to 1962, when he returned to the West Indies, he taught in Ghana and started a children's theatre. He is now teaching History at the University of the West Indies and has recently completed a thesis at the University of Sussex on Jamaican Slave and Creole Society in the eighteenth century. His previous books include *Four Plays for Primary Schools* (1964), *Odale's Choice* (A play, 1967), and the trilogy of long poems: *Rights of Passage* (1967), *Masks* (1968), and *Islands* (1969).

EDWIN MORGAN was born in Glasgow in 1920. He served with the Royal Army Medical Corps (1940–46), mainly in the Middle East – Egypt, Palestine, Lebanon. In 1947 he took his M.A. at Glasgow University, where he teaches English at the moment. He has always been interested in languages and has translated a number of foreign poets, i.e. Montale, Mayakovsky, Voznesensky, and József. He became interested in concrete poetry in 1962 and has had concrete and visual poems included in various international exhibitions and anthologies. He has recently written the libretto for a new opera, *The Charcoal-Burner*, commissioned by the B.B.C. in Scotland. His volume of poems *The Second Life* (1968) was awarded the Cholmondeley Prize for poetry in that year, and also a Scottish Arts Council Publication Prize. His other books include *The Vision of Cathkin Braes* (1952), *Beowulf* [translation into modern English verse] (1962), *The Cape of Good Hope* (1955), *Poems from Eugenio Montale* (1959), *Sovpoems* (1961), (editor) *Collins Albatross Book of Longer Poems* (1963), *Starryveldt* (1965), *Emergent Poems* (1967), *Gnomes* (1968), (co-editor) *Scottish Poetry* 1–4 (1966–69).

Penguin Modern Poets

15

ALAN BOLD

EDWARD BRATHWAITE

EDWIN MORGAN

Penguin Books

Penguin Books Ltd, Harmondsworth, Middlesex, England
Penguin Books Inc., 7110 Ambassador Road, Baltimore, Maryland 21207, U.S.A.
Penguin Books Australia Ltd, Ringwood, Victoria, Australia

—

This selection first published 1969

—

Copyright © Penguin Books Ltd, 1969

—

Made and printed in Great Britain by
C. Nicholls & Company Ltd
Set in Monotype Garamond

Contents

5

CONTENTS

Acknowledgements

For permission to reprint copyright material the following acknowledgements are made: for poems by Alan Bold from *To Find the New* (1967) and *A Perpetual Motion Machine* (1969) to Chatto and Windus Ltd; for poems by Edward Brathwaite from *Rights of Passage* (1967), *Masks* (1968) and *Islands* (1969) to Oxford University Press; for poems by Edwin Morgan from *The Second Life* (1968) to the Edinburgh University Press, from *The Vision of Cathkin Braes* (1952) to William MacLellan, Glasgow and for the poems 'Not Playing The Game' and 'After The Party' to the *New Statesman*; 'The Flowers of Scotland' to *Scottish International*; 'Frontier Story' to the *Listener*; 'For Bonfires' and 'Floating off to Timor' to Glasgow University Literary Society and the Editors of *Epos* and *Phoenix*; 'Phoning' to *Lines Review;* and for 'Drift' to *Ambit.*

ALAN BOLD

Recitative

(*to Ronald Stevenson*)

Come, let's away to prison;
We two alone will sing like birds i' the cage.
                                    Shakespeare: *King Lear*
Whereas a man may have noon audience,
Noght helpeth it to tellen his sentence.
                        Chaucer: *Prologue to The Nun's Priest's Tale*

You ask a poet to sing
Why
Even the birds are hoarse.
The nightingale that long ago
Numbed Keats, is dead.
What of the wind whispering through the trees
When no one cares to hear?
Perhaps you think –
'Ah! the golden skinned lassies
Can still move a poet.'

Once I sang
But that was before I knew
What went on in the world.
Yes! I was blithe,
Chirping away happily,
And, like Chauntecleer, closing my eyes
To do it.
I was, however, ignoring
The modern world
With all its blessings
And all its faults.
When I saw gestant China

Bear well – I rejoiced,
But did not sing.
Could I ignore the toll of the struggle?

Damn it!
Our voices are not made for singing now
But for straight-talking.
As the sea-surge turns over more filth
We may do some good
By exposure.
Look at the moon tonight
Or at the sea.
But before an easy praise of nature
Reflect on those folk
Who have not our sensitive thoughts,
For whom bread, not words, is life:
They matter.

Song implies melody; but the poet
Is after harmony,
Speaking for myself.
Songs have been sung
And dances have been danced
And slaves have done the singing
And peasants have done the dancing
To lessen their hell.
It may be that after this
When people are really allowed
To live,
The birds will sing afresh,
And then the poets will join them.
But for the present
We have enough songs that lie
Unsung.

Most of them by great singers.
Our job is to try
To change things.
After Hiroshima
You ask a poet to sing?

Cause and Effect

He thought before the war
Of conflicts, heroism, enemies
Who had to be crushed;
Causes that had to be fought for.

He had no time before the war
For bright skies, fields, the warm
Sun, his woman – only
Causes that had to be fought for.

I see him now after the war
In my lifetime. I notice his love
Of the sun, bright skies, fields, his woman:
Causes that have to be fought for.

Two Scientific Sonnets
From *The Tomb of David Hume*

THE TWO CULTURES

The Trifid Nebula to my green eyes
Looks like an aged pundit gazing down
At worlds of mortals; I see a frown
And tilted head and folded hands; a wise

Old meditating gentleman who tries
To do his best but gets weary. A crown
Of stars suspended to his left; a gown
Of white silk wrapped round him. He nods and sighs.

I know I see like this because I use
A heritage of seeing to direct
All shapes into a schematic pattern.

I know that man's great task is to unlearn
These modes of seeing, that he must expect
The unexpected. But what does he lose?

SIX DIMENSIONS

We move in five dimensions you must know:
First, revolving; second, orbiting the sun;
Third, tied to the sun in unearthly slow
Galactic revolution; fourth, the one

That splits astronomers, our rapid flight
From other galaxies; and fifth, the way
We walk about on earth – the speed of light
Not being in our picture of the day.

But I believe there is another trace
Of movement that has some significance
To our minute position in all space:

This is a moving dependent on chance.
It is the way a look, a touch, can give
An absolute necessity to live.

Astro Graph the Artist

We, I think, should again turn to the working artist to learn what actually happens when somebody makes an image. What use does he make of tradition, what difficulties does he encounter?

E. H. Gombrich: *Meditations on a Hobby Horse*

A long shaft of sunlight fell on the head
Of Astro Graph and as he woke, he yawned
And thought, 'Twelve o'clock and still in bed.
Ah well, just like Burns – never to be found
At sunrise.' He then slumped over with a sound
Like canvas tearing. As he began to snore
Thought, 'I'll get up when I'm ready, not before.'

Astro Graph the artist had a law
That justified belief, in his own mind.
Whenever he did something that he saw
As stupid he would ruminate to find
An aberration of a similar kind
In a great artist. 'You don't really expect'
He would say, 'to find great artists perfect.'

He couldn't find a shilling for the gas
Which made him Rembrandt who had little sense
Of keeping money. Carbuncles on his arse
Placed him alongside Marx. And when agents
From Bond Street declined his latest immense
Painting he was neglected like Van Gogh
Or learning pain and suffering like Sholokhov.

Astro had a talent; that was true.
But it was almost incidental and

Had slept for years. Picasso in his blue
Period, of course, had burned some work. In grand
Style Astro did the same. He was in the band
Of eremites, artists who must 'die to life'
For art, like Thomas Mann. Replica of the knife

That did for Marlowe's life was always carried
By Astro just in case he needed blood
For his last letter-poem (he had not married
The author of *My Life* but said he would,
Like Essenin, die for her). In this mood
He had to tell the world that though his heart
Was bleeding he had left, for all, his art.

As the cut opened to the knife he had
A flash of insight. All he had to give
Was true and now he saw why Blok was sad,
Wagner bitter. But he would have to live
To express this. Our last alternative
Turned towards the mirror on his shelf
And saw, for the first time, only himself.

A Real Vision

My favourite slice of time
Is early evening
In summer when the buildings fade
Away under the all pervasive red.
Sound recedes too and in a sense
Becomes a lively silence,
A lovely kind of silence.

It is then I am aware
Before the first sight of the first star
Of what my city gives to me
That I refuse to see.
Is there anything in the world
Like green leaves glittering gold?
Or so intense
As the trance
That holds the spectator
As the red and blue begin to scatter
From cloud to cloud
And dominate the mood?

And every night the glow
Is changed to give a different show.
Is it possible to wish for dusk
As the sun becomes a crimson disc
Burning through the atmosphere
In the grandeur of our nearest, dearest star?
Look then at the afterglow
Converting all belief to awe.

At other times it is impossible to share
The extremity of the glare

That would destroy your sight with beauty
A vicious shade of beauty.

One evening I watched swing
Across the sky, a hundred birds on the wing
Cascading and diving within the trail,
Swooping and ducking, and all
Observing in general the shape
Of their overall flying ship.
Faster and fiercer than fish
And free as the air through which they crash.
Intellectually humble you might say;
But it is we who sigh.

On a still night, the quiet
Lets the clouds hang about
And like great luxurious potentates
They bask in gold the sun creates.

Or one delicate wisp drifts
Reluctantly along as the wind shifts.

White brush strokes on a blue ground,
Cirrus clouds live furthest from the source of planetary
        sound.
Underneath the long elegant stratus
Frames the glorious solar apparatus.

At last the low slung shreds
Of water vapour stirred with reds
On their purple underbellies
Hovered between the various blues
Above, and yellow-pink below
Finally gives to grey.

Everything turns round this sun
Within our solar system
And how resentfully we revolve
Into the cold and dark half
We recognize as night,
A hiatus I could learn to hate
For keeping me, until its next birth,
From the most astonishing sight on earth.

That's Life?

Far from the scent of the crocus
And the pavanne of Scottish daffodils
A loud crash was heard in Princes Street.
Safe from the steady gaze
Of the grey carrara marble Scott
A jabbering unknown tramp had died.
One could certainly doubt it
But the blood was fresh
Enough to say he lived
Once. A peering crowd of blanket faces
Did not ponder if he loved,
Or had been loved, instead
They wondered at how far ahead
In life they were. Were they *more*
Than one rung up the ladder of life?
Yet their strange obsession with his death
Charged it with more meaning than his life.
Were they in any way superior
To the thing within
Old and tattered clothes?
Who in that smiling crowd would want
To guess beside the loud
Crash of buses, private cars and men
A solitary member of the human race had died
And not diminished life?
And if they had been the one
Would anything have stopped?
Being apart from them
It was not, they thought, a part
Of them. And when policemen took the few
Details of the case, facts

Conveyed to them
That the lifeless ones in life
Caused much more trouble than they were worth.
They were wrong: their minds blinded
By a candle flame of thought.
There was a man
But he was bespoken for.

Epitaph for W. B. Yeats

A mystic mind, an age apart,
A man who wished to be a work of art;
An ageing man, a life become a word,
A desire to be an eternal golden bird.

A fear of what confronts one in the glass,
A fear, therefore, of self not soul;
An inability to comprehend the mass,
A false idea of the poetic role.

ALAN BOLD

A Little Sound for Alice

How often it's been raved about before;
The love a woman can exact from one.
How quickly the banal sentiments run
When any man his sword goes through a door,

And does it matter if she is a whore,
An angel or a devil or a nun,
When it comes to the real organic fun?
The water laps each pebble on a shore.

Yet show me female form that I could scorn
And numbered there will certainly not be
A lovely serene face with deep brown eyes

And hair as black as trees against the sky
And head that acts particularly on me:
The earth will one day bear with her her born.

Kafka's Grave

I went to lay a stone on Kafka's grave
In Prague. I wanted to make some gesture.
I wanted to leave something, to be sure
Of posthumous connexion, and thus save

Complete eclipse, invading this enclave
Of total brilliance, foreign anywhere.
In Kaprova Street, the Old Town Square,
Jewish Cemetery, family grave.

And so this wise city with its façades
Obscured, with its great things only perceived
Behind successive layers, its charm in part

Its architectural anarchy, its art
Persistent as pulsating stars, invades
And conquers. Force without physique believed.

Topless Poem
(To Paul Johnson)

When breasts are bared, empires crumble:
Shattered is the mystique of *tradition*:
(That insidious coalescence
Of anachronism, obsolescence, and expediency).
Crowned heads and racketeers wilt
And squirm at the spectacle of a nipple
Displayed naturally – without smut
Or titillation.
And the whores with breasts like prunes
Balk as shop girls and female factory workers
Point their bonny bosoms outwards.
While the plastic women of Japan
Scream their anger at mammary freedom
Foam plastic from their frontal globes –
Or simply acquiesce.

But the economic structure
Whence this fashion comes
Rests secure.
For a little while longer
Some men indulge themselves
With nihilistic natter about bust lines.

To support a Socialist order
Lacking empathy
With those who make up that order,
Is simply to sip South African Sherry
And damn Apartheid.

Profile

The working classes have 'coorse' faces,
Blunt features, and noses like nothing in Van Dyck;
There is nothing elegant, no English roses,
And little to recommend them, like
Fineness of character, they've none,
Or impeccable honesty – it wouldn't be worth while.
They are even deficient in colouring, the sun
Was not enough to compensate the vile
Food supply that nourished them. That's why I say:
A little bit of Nietzsche goes a long, long way.

A Memory of Death

Nineteen fifty-six was a momentous year,
The year of Suez and Hungary and the death
Of my father. I was thirteen. He was forty-nine.
His body stiffened in the quarry for a day or so,
His flesh submerged and became bloated
While I sat at home full of premonitions of his death.
It seemed the most natural thing for him to die,
The fitting conclusion to the warnings
And daily visits from genial policemen.
Four days we waited, then the news. Dead.
Found dead in the quarry. Circumstances unknown.
Cause of death: asphyxia due to drowning.

'William Bold/ Clerk of Works/ (Dept. of Agric. for Scot.)/
... 1956/ March/ Found drowned in Bigbreck Quarry,/
Twatt, Birsay, about 4.30 p.m. on Sunday 18th/ March
1956. Last seen alive about 6.30 p.m. on/ Wednesday 14th
March 1956...'

I remember how the letters to my mother brought back
That summer on the farm in Orkney. The cabin,
The cottage. Living between the cabin and the cottage.
It was the one time I had him to myself.
On the farm Hazel used to take me in her bed at night.
I clung to her big body and felt her warm
Limbs. Hazel was kind and rather slow
And she never said much. But each night
She let me share her bed to get the warmth.
She could dribble warm milk down my mouth,
Drive a tractor and decapitate
A hen. Only she could milk the cows expertly,
Gripping their udders with her weather-beaten hands

Laughing as if she had everything anyone could want.
Her presence gave me comfort like a field of corn,
Her voice familiar as the motors threshing,
As the dogs running and barking. Once,
I fell in the cowshed. I stank
With the sloppy excrement plastered all over.
But she threw her big-boned torso round me,
Washed me down and grasped me and smiled
And the sun shone through her mane of hair.
On the same cow she sat me and held me tight.
And at night we would gape at the moon
Silently fixing our thoughts on it, Hazel
With her arms round me, smiling, glowing,
And we would go to bed after porridge and cocoa.

'I can't tell you how sorry I am to hear of your sad loss . . . I
pray that God be with you to give you strength to bear
your great loss.'

Snick-crack! The shot was fired. Whirr
Of wings and beat of leaves and shadows in the night.
My first time pulling the trigger. The lake.
Undulating blackness catching shreds of light.
I giggled with the sensation of accomplishment.
He winked and grinned. Then into the boat.
Silently we sliced through the black water.
We didn't speak but listened to the ripples.
Then the illegal otter was launched: a length
Of rope decorated with murderous hooks and, sleek
As an otter, the streamlined wood that pulled the rope.
We waited, looking at each other, grinning
Conspiratorially. Then the jerk and pull
And rip! The mouth snaps and the lip pouts
And we've got a trout. A gleaming trout, a trout
Of subtle highlights and I thump its lovely head

Hard against an oar. One down and several
To go. It's up to us. No rush. Our choice.
Guilty – and happy. Cold – but flushed. Two – like one.
At the farm we grilled the trout. They sizzled away
And we slobbered after them. He thumbed to me.
'He'll make a good poacher, this one, some day!'
Cosy and lovable farm, in an hour or so the sun
Will show. The lake will sparkle and we can look
But no one else will know.

'How is Alan? I suppose he will soon be giving work a
thought as well. What a shame to think he doesn't have his
Dad to start him off & such a clever man.'

Fiddle music, stomping feet, thrills
Whisky flowing, boozed up to the gills,
Children on the floor and cakes,
Party pieces, old repeated jokes.

Laughter linking kids and wives and daft
Workers clumping joyously on soft
Carpets – kisses innocent as sweets
Embraces making boys and girls mates.

Secrets shared and little stories told
Peat thrown on the fire against the cold.
An old piano, floorboards worn and dark
And folk united through the heavy work.

It finishes too soon, the morning calls
And blankets cover all internal ills.
A passer-by will see another farm
Oblivious to the life that breaks the storm.

And inside as the shutters shake and creak
A child's eyes eagerly wait for day to break

And look hard for another night like this
Hoping to God the present doesn't pass.

'I never for one minute thought Bill would come to such
an end I always admired his carefree personality ... God
knows best and that's all we can say about it.'

A lot has been written about Skara Brae,
Vivid first-hand impressions made on the spot.
Full of mystery or a stern sense of history,
Or perhaps some blots scrawled on the back of a postcard
In the pub.
I have a feeling for the place now, rather than a picture.
We had been building a bridge,
Watching the digger devastating the earth,
Waving off the midgies and the clegs.
And after the morning's work: Skara Brae.
I saw burials older than I will ever be.
Remarkable reconstructions of the primitive way of life.
Immaculate patterns of rooms from stone.
The evidence of ingenuity, the suggestion
Of a rigid way of life. And the whole thing
Deep in the ground.
It did not seem amazing or beautiful.
It seemed preposterous in comparison with the farm.
And, perhaps worst of all, it was invaded by new people,
Empty of the old inhabitants. I remember thinking that.
I often think of it now as a silent tomb
For those we never could have known and never try
To know. He was there and it sticks now.
It is redolent with memorial melodies,
A monument made from destruction.
And when I saw Skara Brae
In that clear afternoon, my muscles aching,
I saw it as a member of posterity.

'... although he was only a lodger his tragic death has
upset me terrible. As you know he was his own worst
friend he certainly was indulging in spirits too much ... all
we can do is bless him from the bottom of our hearts and
remember his happy smile.'

I remember his happy smile.
I remember the gaps of missing teeth, the black
Spots on the white, the large lower lip,
I remember the fairisle pullover, green and rust
And white, the ruddy face, the twisted arm broken
In a car crash. I remember the way he walked
Like a big ape
His jacket open, flapping, his eyes bright.

I remember too the alcoholic breath, the false
Euphoria and, after tumbling into chasms of distress,
Depression and confessions of guilt.
These no longer matter, though they seemed to matter
    then.
They mattered more than they should have. It is so
In Scotland, land of the omnipotent No.

The Sunday-school picnic, the twittering old birds,
The benevolent boy-scouts, the ministers dripping
With goodwill. And the disgrace. He was drunk.
Not objectionable. Just dead drunk.
Sprawled out on the grass focusing on the sky,
With whispers hissing maliciously round about.
They were well pleased with something to feel superior
About, with half a chance to gloat.
'Do you mind Mr Bold?' What! Grunt!
'Do you mind Mr Bold not lying there?' Mmmm!
'Do you think you could stand up?'
He tried to, tried so hard, so ostentatiously,

Arms working like a tightrope walker's,
Legs unbuckling – then thump.
Down and out.

'. . . it was a huge shock to us all after being here so long
with us he was in here so short before having a talk with
Jim my husband and the rest of them it was a cold day and
I made tea to them all sitting round the fire I think he
missed the cabin as they all used to call it he could take a
rest when he wanted . . .'

He left the land rover
And stared deep into the water
Thinking life offered nothing more than this liquid pit.
Everything shrunk to the need for action,
For decision. And the audacity of the stars.
Everything at such a distance, people, family,
Friends. And headlong he fell
Slowly into the water
And swore in bubbles
And his eyelids filled with blackness.

A Moral Tale

In the freezing North Bridge the other night
While the wind howled the dry leaves off the street,
A young thing in a short skirt with a sweet
Line in curves stumbled for the bus – right

At the wrong moment. First a flash of white
Buttocks then brown stocking tops. How her neat
Legs scuffed against the ground, and how the heat
Scorched her knees. It was really quite a sight.

At the bus stop watching, two tough old bags
Dangled from some folded arms. 'That skirt
Was *far* too short' the clam-like mouth that sags

Said. 'And underneath the little flirt
Was hardly decent!' They smiled in nodding spite
The hags. 'Oh yes,' at last, 'it served her right.'

Old Nell

An old woman died near me. An old get
You would call her – slobbering and timid
In face of real power, yes. And yet
Arrogant with her proud tongue before
Those closest to her. Can you imagine?
Her friends thought her a fiendish old hag.
'She'll give it them' they would say.
'They'll be wary of tackling that steep crag.'
When she was young and, so I hear,
Lovely and desirable with wild shocks
Of hair and a shape as nice as clear
Skies – when she was very young
Her voice could charm the birds and her young lads
Would slumber in a lullaby of lust and love.
She was cocky with it too and would take
All comers. They tell me there were enough
To sink a battleship. I find this hard
To accept.
When I saw her on wind swept
Mornings shuffling with dropsy blurred
Vision among the piles of dried leaves
I laughed. She couldn't frighten a field mouse
Let alone wield a battle axe. I could not see
The bright young thing hiding in that hideous
Old lined face or standing in bauchles. Honestly,
I tried; but to no purpose. Then
One morning her trembling hands and brown
Old face came near me. When the cracking
Noise emerged from her throat I was scared
To be seen with her. 'Bless you laddie.'
That was all she said. Like you

My defences got to work. I would not be had;
No sentimental fool would take me in.

Once I saw her in a shop complaining
About the change. 'She'll give it them.'
I watched. She capitulated without
A fight. Later I could hear her railing
At her daughter and her son-in-law.
He, the spineless looking sort with pin striped
Double breasted suits (perhaps the ratio
Of deference to power intensified
With the ramifications of the family tree).
They were all struck dumb
While the ignorant old woman viciously
Abused them. Butter wouldn't melt
In her mouth – it would boil!
But, I was told, if you decried the old girl
To the young ones, they would spoil for a fight,
Blood being thicker than water. Well,
To cut a long story short, and I suppose
That every year of her withered life
Told a story or, at least, one of those
Anecdotes you hear: 'Guess what!
Old Nell turned that sparrow faced swine
On the street.' Or, 'You should have
Heard her when they said another bun
Was in the oven! And that spiv
Of a son-in-law living off the dole.
Think they could think of something better
To do all day. He's had his hole
So many times, that young brute,
That there won't be nothing left.'
Cackling laughter. I had none of it
Being in my teens, but when she died

I had that agenbite of inwit.
So old and alone and yet once so brave
Battling against superiors – in the end
It was too much. Let us face it,
In the beginning it was too much for one.
So while young life can be full for me
I would tread carefully on that 'Bless you laddie.'
As long as they die off old in winter, danger
Can be averted in silent anger.

Your Human Face

Every time I look at you
And you and you and you and you and you
I wonder at the slight smile
That operates your lips.
Is it part of a disguise?
I ask because I doubt
That everybody feels the same way
Although it looks like it.

Some day or night I'll see behind
That confident expression
That tells you have been cured
Of some minor irritation.
Like a novice I would explain
What goes on behind the skin
What particularization you deny
What mechanism you use.

On our small planetary scale
The moon swings around
Presenting the same bland mug.
And we got at her, or him, or it.
It took a long time, long enough to know
That man on earth is not a simple fact.
That only when you have nothing more to hide
Will you permit me to see your other side.

From The Tomb of David Hume
Stanzas 23–24

We have to face up to certain pecadilloes,
Nugatory issues often swept aside,
For in the framing of hypotheses
We guess and try to falsify the guess,
Record sense-data after the creative event
And conjectural cowardice exists
As well as consequential diffidence.
The sun is not immortal
Though suns in general may be
And so we must die the death
As an earthbound species.
Now we matter more than asteroids
Whirling round supporting nothing
But death
Or distant suns collapsing
Centuries ago.
So posterity will hate the coming
End and copy us, as we grotesquely parody
A more hierarchic past, instead
Of acting out the present. The past
Has happened, we create the present
But the future is ahead.
Chemistry is so important.
The conversion of hydrogen into helium
Sounds easy, even common, so easy
It sounds as if we were ill
At ease with science, as if we dangled
Figures for your fun. Do not be fooled.
Life will became rare and then extinct
Because the sun is heating up.

Two or three thousand million years from now
No one will remember us because
There won't be anyone to do
The remembering.
Our sun is too big for us to cope with
And it is going to grow
While we glow and bubble in the oceans
And melt through no fault of our own.
Such a young small star, our sun,
So kind but in the end
Indiscriminately destructive.
In the beginning was hydrogen
And it will outlive men.

How much we make of our metaphysical fiddling
Instead of seeing life as something following
A shower of stars condensing out of clouds of gas
And planets moving, and great suns turning in galaxies.
We anthropomorphize immediate nature
And trivialize the wonder of the earth
By pretending that it dropped ready made
From the fidgeting of a self-made God.
A God! A backward dog! A word this age
Inters itself in. So much superstition
Which reduces the miracle of life
Not enough dissemination of the real.
The important task you set
Of making a meaning out of life
By making it accessible to all
Has been retarded. The Enlightenment
Believed all was possible, all meant
To fall into place like a perfect jigsaw.
The dark Romantic era passionately held
The ultimate unknowability of the world.

Well we know the arrogance
In this belief of humility.
We know we may know everything to know
And what we'll never know we'll never know.
So many people exercise their brains
At the expense of themselves, growing pains
Merely.
How marvellous to see a world beneath a leaf
Or discern a conflict underneath your feet
Among the insect world. This worm
That writhes in pain through the dust
Feels nothing when we patronize.
If anywhere, the message in the skies
Is the real message. How telling
To interpret ourselves as larger
Brighter animals and smile
Indulgently as if the whole thing were a joke.
It is no joke. An avenue of lime trees
Conceals an ant-like universe. Why tease
The meaning to mean more than that?
It is the telescope and the microscope
Not the microscope alone that shall colour
Our vision.
Our earth is four and a half thousand million
Years old and still
The recent life upon it is intent
On self-destruction. There are more
Ingenious ways of imitating suns than blasting
Human beings to obscene fragments.
Our sun is still young
And small, newer than the red giants
Who live a fifteen thousand million year,
The age of our galaxy with its twenty
Cosmic curtsies. But wait:

No birthday presents yet.
We are indifferent to the life
Upon our planet, as a species we
Do not cohere but could.
Human. The universal view
Is something that must come, after you
Achieve a world-view and care
For the sufferings of others, not
Passively and smugly. Active and hot.
A supernova does not exist
For a child of the Indian lower-caste
Girl, because the child will not get past
Its second year. The way it twists
Its face in pain tells you
As if you didn't know
That nothing is inside its mind
But food
That should
Be in its blood.

A Night's Dream

Her gestures tumble clichés round the room
Filled with examining eyes, while
The pungent stench of cheap perfume
Obscures the blank aftermath of a smile.

In the dark when the light had been fucked off,
I read by my bulbous flame
The story of my life, as if the same
Old fanny had produced a spark,
A fusion of all that glistered in my loins,
Ears, balls, knees and thrusting arse.
It started with a theme –
I call it that – made
Of memories of a randy boy.
Marx only knows the feelings that I had
When all the other lads, my pals,
Kicked footballs in the streets,
Streets filled with paper and with dung,
They wanted to kick balls,
I wanted to rest mine in a cunt
And spinning from the first attempt
To draw the spunk myself
I then remembered Nancy's tits
Big, beautiful, spear–
Pointed breasts that trembled in my hands
Like perfect jellies.
She was not the first I'd felt
But then she was the best.

In the privacy of the open night
One male grasshopper drove
His point home with a quick shove
And the lady's shudder. Love?

Sir Humphry Davy (1778–1829)

As well as being a chemist
Sir Humphry Davy was a poet,
And his friend Coleridge said to him:
'Humph, take this science and stow it.

Your poetry's going to rack and ruin
And Southey thinks that's very bad;
He has anthologized you
And to ignore that is mad.

Please lay off this useless science
And let us be sublime.
Utilize your language with
An imagination like mine.

I tell of my Christabel,
My Mariner, and Kubla Khan,
And you reply with nitrous oxide
A "laughing gas" no use to man.

Can it help me to write good poetry?
No! and what's the use, old son,
Of sodium, potassium, calcium,
Barium, magnesium and strontium?'

While Samuel rambled on and on
Humphry studied fire-damp.
And to stop death by explosion
Invented a safety lamp.

Second Thoughts

No we won't forget what you did
Although we have no way, you say, of knowing
How you did it. Or even why you did.
Through the bloody wet
Slow slushy ground you trod for us, you say.
Is that right? Is that what you say? Well
It's true we can't complain the way you
Could. Oh no. We've never lived outside the womb
Since we've been blessed with this blessed bomb.
We younger folk can't feel the quick snap
Of shrapnel biting at our legs, or yet the pain
Of brutal parting from . . . but you *know* so much.
So much. Too strong to cry. The choke
That hides the tears the strong man always hides,
(You told us so), begs
The questions; was it a clear choice that Tom
Dick and Harry made to fight to sing a song
Of freedom, or was he merely slugged with fear
Of his superiors? Not *for* his country;
Because of it?
Was it merely the slimy quirk of quite
Arbitrary circumstance that made him clasp the cause
Of anti-fascism? I would like this grit,
This latent pearl of wisdom, cultured.
Is there a chance that,
Give or take a birth, a place to spawn,
Our boys, you good old boys,
May have served on Hitler's side?
Have you nothing in you that grumbles?
Absolutely *nothing* to hide?

The reason for our smile is reason
Clipped and passed on, tried
Against fanaticism, the eyeless worm
That slithers in attrition in the mud
And, hardly seen, acquires a double load.
If this is true, then I for one
Do not accept the code of deference to
The men whom thoughtful men put first.
It's not enough to do it once
By accident. It's not enough
To be right by default.
The reason knows no indivisible
Divisions, the reason knows
No reason for your subsequent decline.
If you remember to remember
What it meant for them, if you remember
All the pain and how it stopped then – no
We won't forget what you did.

De Profundis

'Man is a tool-making animal.' Benjamin Franklin

1

Day after day the soldiers came to see
The hole in the ground. That is, after we
In the village were treated from the blast
That came the first day. Just where the old tree

2

Of the village stood, near the coast line where
The waves rocked back and forwards and the air
Bit into human flesh, the flames appeared
And spread towards our houses till the glare

3

Told our own bombers that a strike had been
Made. Only a small warning to the green
Hills of our country, they affirmed. In fact,
Few were hurt. It would be being mean

4

With human life to have complained that some
Friends close to us would be ghoulishly dumb
For good. In the pamphlets circulated
Around the village, there was a too glum

5

Prediction of the numbers they expected
Dead, or those, so badly mutilated
That their bodies would be burned in oil
At a safe distance from a strictly stated

6

Boundary. And while the crumbling white foam
Crumbled in the harbour and the spume
From the trawlers was carried out to sea
The frogmen came with equipment to comb

7

The coast line in case there might be some things
To explain a sudden attack. Rings
Of barbed wire now surrounded the deep hole,
The gaping belly where the first soundings

8

Were made. At first the doctors could not say
What caused the burns. At last they said the grey
Faces of those afflicted had been caused
By shock. But when the skin peeled like damp clay

9

From an armature, they began to go
More deeply into their stories. Also,
No country had been identified
As an aggressor; therefore there was no

10

Question of retaliation. Men
Who had seen the blast had drooled, shaken
By the sight, of a huge black creature
Breathing fire that had crashed out from a den

11

Deep in the earth where heat was constantly
Appropriate for its hellish hide. If we

Were frightened by these stories, the scientists
Were worse. 'The End of Man's Ascendancy

12

In Sight' the headlines, inches deep, exclaimed
When news got to the press. And then they blamed
The politicians who had 'let the rot
Of man go on'. Churches said the damned

13

Could be identified and the creature
Was the devil merely overdue,
And that it was certainly time to choose
One's denomination. 'You can be sure,'

14

The Pope intoned in St Peter's Square,
'That those strongest in faith need have no fear.
Others are welcome to our bulging flock
But remember – this is no once a year

15

Offer, it is the chance of a lifetime.'
The Archbishop of Canterbury, slime
On his brogues after coming to the scene
Of the incident, began his speech: ' "Home

16

Is where one starts from " said our national poet,
And I agree. We did not, could not, know it
But God had decided to make a sign
Before *our* eyes – so that we would believe it.'

17

In our village, many wearied of those –
Clerics, politicians, generals – whose prose
Blanketed out our air with platitudes
And auguries. But then the monster rose

18

One day from that profound hole in the ground
And roared. 'For centuries a human sound
Was enough to frighten us from the hard
Surface of the earth. My colleagues have drowned

19

Their sorrows in your lochs or underneath
Your feet. Man *was* supreme. The laurel wreath
Was well deserved for that huge brain that made
A heaven on the earth. And now both

20

Our species cannot share it. You have made
A nuclear world of light and pretty red
Flames too hot for you. We will succeed
When your own efforts see your species dead.'

A Little Bird Told Me

A blackbird landed on my window-sill.
God! It was cold enough to make you hate!
'You live in an age more obdurate
Of feeling than the snow; the harshest pill

To swallow is like whisky to the chill
That emanates from your neurotic state;
The ethos of a race that can equate
Health with social atrophy is nil.'

The peroration gave me no surprise.
The bird had spoken out, or I had in.
A vision of millions of men, I knew,

In happiness, would not impress the few
Who people this small island and who win
By cutting out their hearts to spite their eyes.

Academic Angst

Be sure that you go to the author to get at *his* meaning, not to find
yours.

John Ruskin: *Sesame and Lilies.*

Phed leans towards me
With a puzzled smile twitching
On his lips.
He leans towards me
And unclicks the polished leather bag
Of books glued to his right
Hand.
He leans towards me
And points to the khaki pages
Of a book of eighteenth century verse.
He reads
After clearing his throat
And tightening his tie
With a sharp and gritty voice.
He reads of money grubbing
Writers
Sycophantic poets
Ostentatious dedications
Slimy and squalid
Selfish hacks.
But it is all
Undeniably beautiful
Undeniably beautiful.
Phed scratches
His worried head
And says: 'You see,
I told you so, then
They were the same

Lickspittles and shoe-shiners
Grubby satellites
Orbiting petty
Little worlds.'
He told me so, it's true
But it is all
Undeniably beautiful
Undeniably beautiful
As if a change of time or name
Could make it other than the same.

The Event
For William Redgrave, for his sculptured triptych, 'The Event'

I

How did it happen, this event?
This silent coalescence, captured and exposed.
Their panic, their ephemeral glance,
Their simulation of indifference
Preserved. Clutching and huddling, forced
To face the judgement of a world they represent.

How did it happen, this event?
This timeless spatial portrait of an age.
The eyes screwed up with doubts
The accusing shouts
Directed at the latest useful grudge.
And that woman's fear: is that meant?

How did it happen, this event?
Are these creatures kin or separate?
Do we read them as lies
Do we sympathize
Do we know what we see and ooze hate?
Or do we see this as some alien element?

2

You would never get *people* to pose
Like this. Not for a fortune.
They want the flattering patina
Of schematic beauty, they want
To click neatly, like clips, into
A pre-existing smirk. They want to be loved.

They want the wide clear eyes, the neck
Curving gracefully like a swan's, the hair
Either perfect or slightly out of place
After the best fashion: there must
Be a precedent. But instead
To get three old men bawling out
Their sordid future, to get liquid only
From a bottle of booze, or light
Only from a cigar. . . . Nobody is *really*
Like that. Or so they say. But look:
There is a child.
A child, the prime creation, pointing.
Dare we follow to where we want
To go? Only the child points
To a new context, to something beyond
That clinging ambience of bronze.
Only a child? And we murder children,
Teaching them to learn the limitations
Of a world of man-made limitations.

      It all looks solid, but that only means
Electromagnetic forces have atoms in their grip
So tightly that they oscillate
About fixed propositions.
And the left side of our brain
Commands our right appendages
To shape out, from the imagination
Of the physical, a purely mental
Pattern, so the atoms become flesh,
Flesh becomes breasts, lips,
Fingers, finely finished form.
We see nothing but what we want
To see: intimations of the viscera
Appal us. Yet only in creation
Can we atone for the great crime of complicity

In the familiar daily death
By intention.
        Perhaps the only meaningful event
Is suicide. Thousands think so.
To contemplate our planet's future
When the sun swallows us somehow
Empties it of all significance. But a child
Points and a child is the living gamble
In a future. And for that child
Our creation of the future exists
Not in our own likeness, but in a greater one.
This is the reason and the consequence of the event,
The gathering together of our physical resources.
Yes, there are ugly faces, bashed features, murderers,
There is endless violence, greed, terror, death.
But this is the material from which we have
To sculpt what comes next. And there is love
To mount it on. And a child points.

3

Only for a while do we think
Reflect – then walk away
And shut out from our consciousness
The only thing that matters in this day.

This is an event too, this power
Of men and women bravely to dismiss
The vital things as artefacts
And never see the corpse they kiss.

From Baudelaire's Le Voyage

6

'O infantile intellects!
We will not spare you the most important thing yet.
Without spotlighting its ubiquitous presence
From the heights to the bottom of the deadly pit,
We saw the tiresome display of immortal sin:

Woman, that vile slave of slaves, strutting and stupid,
In love with herself, not seeing the obscene joke;
Man that gutsy tyrant, bawdy, brutal, and damned
Inhibited – a sewer with its gutter choked;

The hangman happy in his work, the martyr's tears,
The formal luncheons dished up and paid for in blood;
The poison of power dictating the dictator,
And the masses embracing the exploiting whip;

Several religions similar to our own,
All with a cheap ticket to heaven; holiness
Getting its satisfaction from nails and hair-shirts
Like a sybarite sprawling in a feather bed;

Prating humanity drunk with its own genius,
And crazy now, though this madness is nothing new,
Screaming to a God, in ferocious agony:
"O my double, O you my master, I curse you!"

And the not-so-stupid, bold lovers of madness,
Eschewing the great herd tied to society,
And losing themselves in opium's great cosmos –
Such is the news of the entire world *every* day.'

In A Second-hand City Bookshop

Life enters here every day to buy and sell
To blow on one dusty volume and recoil
From lumps of spider's web upon another.
Heads arch stiffly backwards in a spell
Of concentration; sharply one pair of teeth
Grates together in annoyance: its loyal
Owner racks the rows while optimism sheds
Its hope of the great discovery among the stuffy shades.

Squeezed spine by spine the titles wait
The archness of a brow that anticipates
A find. The bibliophilic passion comes alive
Only if the specimen is denied to someone else; to create,
In this field, as in others, is to steal. A visceral
Commotion confirms the scoop and thus Yeats
Becomes the value of a first edition – much much more
Is paid than when the poems appeared in 1904.

That's a big day, though, and much more common
Is the tiny lady who goes round and round the floor
Embezzling all the warmth inside in winter. She
Prefers the second-hand and used because the parchment on
Her bones absorbs the desiccation of redundant authors.
It comes for time to leave and as she shuffles to the door
She sticks out sixpence for the cheapest she could hold
And clutches the collection she will burn to beat the cold.

Or the student frowning so to emphasize
Erratic genius. He is conscious that his personality
Is scrutinized by every sentient thing. Every
Movement is exaggerated: muscles jerk, eyes

Jolt within their fleshy orbit, and the face
Puts ingenuity of expression on display.
The scarf flicks forward as he bungles at the table to a halt
(Well worth two and six to make one's presence felt. . . .).

But the fullest sadness rests still in certain books
That are the images of pathos. Each shelf supports
The minor failures, the living dust of countless men
Who trundled all their guts into inactive works.
Not for money in their lifetimes but for a world
Equipped to understand the sacrifice of great hearts.
And thus they leave to others the lighting of a dawn
That will forever fade as the waste goes on.

Immolation

The reflection of a distortion becomes a distorted reflection.
Georg Lukács

In the street where the cobbles still survive
And the huge tenements hang above
Dictating terms to you;
Where the gutters gurgle in the rain
Large puddles form, and to the eye
Of the beholder gleam:
Honest to the hulking stone
That holds tight a score
Of families. When the storm ceases
The undulations in the cobbles drain,
Full of rain water no longer
Clean, but muddy and still
When the wind rises to a whisper.
Into this
It is possible to read
Your own shape, and, in the background,
The black rocky image
Cutting up the white sky.
Silhouetted thus, the context
May appear static and eternal and just,
But if you spit
Into the puddle or, better still,
Drop in a match
The ripples
Fracture
The tall oppressive backdrop.

On the one hand
You have a picture of what exists

About you, as it is –
Silent and classically rational even.
But see how easy it is
To spit or, better still, to drop
A lighted match
Into that image, that mirage. It takes
Some considerable time
To start a smoke haze
And I would hope
To be there when
The eyes, brains and hands
Piece together a new
Jigsaw puzzle or crazy
Paving if you like
From the rubble that remains.

Eng. Soc. Lit.

As long as a man assumes that the evils of this earth have their cause in the specific failures of individual persons and individual institutions, he still remains in the stage of intellectual childhood.

Günther Blöker: *The New Realities*

This is the era of the understatement
When parlour pundits etch the age in prose.
A thousand million columns now propose
To give some reason for U.S. containment,

Or air an instant conscience. Entertainment
Is the aim. And this only shows
That paucity of Leninism grows
Into apotheosis of debasement.

'Left-wingers' do not constitute a threat
To Capital or its proliferation.
And yet it is desirable to hate

The thing that draws them to the second nation:
Their Marxism was a brief flirtation:
Just petting, no deep penetration.

The Realm of Touching

Between my lips the taste of nighttime blends
And then dissolves. It is blank as my eyelids close.
For a flickering of time I concentrate on how time ends.

It should be present, the scent of the rose
We bought, though one petal has begun to fall.
Somehow that simplifies the girl I chose.

Night music must be the sweetest sound of all.
It is made to overwhelm with virtuosity.
But every night it is the same pounding on the same wall.

Nocturnal images are said to be the ones that stay
Longest, with exploitation of the dark half-tone.
This I disregard and watch for the day.

A touch in the realm of touching alone
Adds presence to the absence of light.
A clasp of hands, then bodies, my own
And hers is when I welcome the blindness of night.

Headlines

As you look around this morning
At the people scudding past
Take a long hard look at someone
For this look may be your last.

There's a resting place on the cooker
There's an opening in the wrists
There's a clean break in the rope
That the factory girl twists.

There's a general realization
That death fits like a glove
On the fingers of a rotting corpse
And claims the one you love.

When you're happy with your sweetheart
When you have all you want at last
Then you fret for the loss of the present
And your future mocks your past.

No apparent reason
For the blade, for the overdose
Of aspirins that crumble
Like the life they bring to a close.

The faces of the children
Smile and stare ahead
And the terrible illusion
Justifies the dead.

When the body of a woman
With everything to lose

Is found on fitted carpets
This suicide is news.

But the suicide by helplessness
The suicide that kills
Anyone who dares to live
In squalor affords no thrills.

Only the dark dark spaces
In the mind that looks around
And fills itself with horror
Are processed, stuffed and crowned.

In the dark of newer nations
That have no nationhood
Killing becomes a commodity
Paid cheaply for in blood.

And at home we watch vicariously
On the telly all the wars
And genocidal conflicts
And polish up our cars.

We have no reason for dying
As we carve the Sunday joint
Someone, somewhere, is crying:
That, surely, is the point.

June 1967 at Buchenwald

The stillness of death all around the camp was uncanny and intolerable.
Bruno Apitz: *Naked Among Wolves*

This is the way in. The words
Wrought in iron on the gate:
JEDEM DAS SEINE. Everybody
Gets what he deserves.

The bare drab rubble of the place.
The dull damp stone. The rain.
The emptiness. The human lack.
JEDEM DAS SEINE.
JEDEM DAS SEINE.
Everybody gets what he deserves.

It all forms itself
Into one word: Buchenwald.
And those who know and those
Born after that war but living
In its shadow, shiver at the words.
Everybody gets what he deserves.

It is so quiet now. So
Still that it makes an absence.
At the silence of the metal loads
We can almost hear again the voices,
The moaning of the cattle that were men.
Ahead, acres of abandoned gravel.
Everybody gets what he deserves.

Wood, beech wood, song
Of birds. The sky, the usual sky.

A stretch of trees. A sumptuous sheet
Of colours dragging through the raindrops.
Drizzle loosening the small stones
We stand on. Stone buildings. Doors. Dark.
A dead tree leaning in the rain.
Everybody gets what he deserves.

Cold, numb cold. Despair
And no despair. The very worst
Of men against the very best.
A joy in brutality from lack
Of feeling for the other. The greatest
Evil, racialism. A man, the greatest good.
Much more than a biological beast.
An aggregate of atoms. Much more.
Everybody gets what he deserves.

And it could happen again
And they could hang like broken carcasses
And they could scream in terror without light
And they could count the strokes that split their skin
And they could smoulder under cigarettes
And they could suffer and bear every blow
And they could starve and live for death
And they could live for hope alone
And it could happen again.
Everybody gets what he deserves.

We must condemn our arrogant
Assumption that we are immune as well
As apathetic. We let it happen.
History is always more comfortable
Than the implications of the present.
We outrage our own advance as beings

By being merely men. The miracle
Is the miracle of matter. Mind
Knows this but sordid, cruel and ignorant
Tradition makes the world a verbal shell.
Everybody gets what he deserves.

Words are fallible. They cannot do
More than hint at torment. Let us
Do justice to words. No premiss is ever
Absolute; so certain that enormous wreckage
Of flesh follows it syllogistically
In the name of mere consistency. In the end
All means stand condemned. In a cosmic
Context human life is short. The future
Is not made, but waits to be created.
Everybody gets what he deserves.

There is the viciously vicarious in us
All. The pleasure in chance misfortune
That lets us patronize or helps to lose
Our limitations for an instant.
It is that, that struggle for survival
I accuse. Let us not forget
Buchenwald is not a word. Its
Meaning is defined with every day.
Everybody gets what he deserves.

Now it is newsprint and heavy headlines
And looking with a camera's eyes.
Now for many it is only irritating
While for others it is absolutely deadly.
No one is free while some are not free.
While the world is ruled by precedent
It remains a monstrous chance irrelevance.
Everybody gets what he deserves.

We turn away. We always do.
It's what we turn into that matters.
From the invisible barracks of Buchenwald
Where only an unsteady horizon
Remains. The dead cannot complain.
They never do. But we, we live.
Everybody gets what he deserves.

That which once united man
Now drives him apart. We are not helpless
Creatures crashing onwards irresistibly to doom.
There is time for everything and time to choose
For everything. We are that time, that choice.
Everybody gets what he deserves.

This happened near the core
Of a world's culture. This
Occurred among higher things.
This was a philosophical conclusion.
Everybody gets what he deserves.

The bare drab rubble of the place.
The dull damp stone. The rain.
The emptiness. The human lack.

EDWARD BRATHWAITE

To Richard, Daofoe and the family at Runaway Bay

EDWARD BRATHWAITE

Libation

Out
of this
bright
sun, this
white plaque
of heaven,
this leaven-
ing heat
of the seven
kingdoms:
Songhai, Mali,
Chad, Ghana,
Tim-
buctu, Volta,
and the bitter
waste
that was
Ben-
in, comes
this shout
comes
this song.

Gong-gongs
throw pebbles in the rout-
ed pools of silence: news
of ripples reach the awakened Zu-
lus: Chaka tastes
the salt blood of the bitter
Congo and all Africa
is one, is whole, nim-

73

tree shaded in Ghana,
in Chad, Mali,
the shores of the cooling kingdoms.

Beat heaven
of the drum, beat
the dark leaven
of the dungeon
ground where buds are wrapped
twist-
ed round dancing shoots. White
salt crackles at root lips, bursts like a fist
and beats out this
prayer:

Nana Firimpong
once you were here
hoed the earth
and left it for me
green rich ready
with yam shoots, the
tuberous smooth of cassava;

take the blood of the fowl
drink
take the *eto*, mashed plantain,
that my women have cooked
eat
and be happy
drink
may you rest
for the year has come round
again.

Asase Yaa,
You, Mother of Earth,
on whose soil
I have placed my tools
on whose soil
I will hoe
I will work
the year has come round
again;

thirsty mouth of the dust
is ready for water
for seed;

drink
and be happy
eat
may you rest
for the year has come round
again.

And may the year
this year of all years
be fruitful
beyond the fruit of your labour:
shoots faithful to tip
juice to stem
leaves to green;

and may the knife
or the cut-
lass not cut
me; roots blunt,
shoots break,
green wither,

winds shatter,
damp rot,
hot harm-

attan come
drifting in harm
to the crops;

the tunnelling
termites not
raise their red

monuments, graves,
above the blades
of our labour. . .

Mmenson

Summon now the kings of the forest,
horn of the elephant,
mournful call of the elephant;

summon the emirs, kings of the desert,
horses caparisoned, beaten gold bent,
archers and criers, porcupine arrows, bows bent;

recount now the gains and the losses:
Agades, Sokoto, El Hassan dead in his tent,
the silks and the brasses, the slow weary tent

of our journeys down slopes, dry river courses;
land of the lion, land of the leopard, elephant
country; tall grasses, thick prickly herbs. Blow elephant

trumpet; summon the horses,
dead horses, our losses: the bent
slow bow of the Congo, the watering Niger . . .

Axum

With the help of the Caliph
of Heaven, who in heaven
and earth conquers all;

I, El Hassan, son of Amida,
King of Axum,
of Halen, Hemer, Rayden and

Salhen,
made war on the Noba;
fought at Takazi, by the ford

of Kemalke;
burnt town, destroyed
villages, pillaging

houses and temples
whether of stone or of straw
did not matter; splattered

blood in the corn;
burnt their altars of horn,
bronze and copper; threw

their dark wooden gods in the river
and the next day moved on
till we reached the Red River . . .

Ougadougou

And I, Ougadougou,
sprawled on the Niger,
watched them come:

red whispering walls moving,
smoke squeezing our eyes,
cinders sneezing. The heat

was before us; mirages danced
in its silver; our brittle walls
crumbled, flat walking roofs

tumbled; red tongues
licked grass from the streets,
children screamed, women ran,

crackled sparks' eyes crashing to ashes;
goats butted and turned, blinded; horses
stamped. Where are the dancers,

the flutes' reed voices
cut from the river, the songs'
achievement of cymbals?

They come riding, porcupine driving
our errors before them; too soft,
too blandished, too ready for peace and for terror.

Timbuctu

Whose gold you carry, camel,
in this cold cold world?
Whose pearls of great price?
Whose cinnamon, whose spice?

Your world of walls, o city
of my birth, rises so certain
so secure; the plains
of dust surrounding us

so kept away, so distant.
Whose gold you carry, camel,
on your hill-top back?
To what far land you now

transport our wealth?
And what wealth here, what
riches, when the gold returns
to dust, the walls

we raised return again
to dust; and what sharp winds,
teeth'd with the desert's sand,
rise in the sun's dry

brilliance where our mosques
mock ignorance, mock pride,
burn in the crackled blaze of time,
return again to whispers, dust.

The Forest

I

Like walls the forest stops us.
Over the ford at Yeji it was waiting:
tangled squat mahogany out-
riders and then the dense, the
dark green tops, bright
shining standing trunks:
wawa, dahoma, esa and
odum; the doom
of the thick stretching green.
Leaves gathered darkness; no
pathway showed the way.
The trunks grew tall and
taller, dark and darker; earth
now damp, fern cool, moss
soft. We hacked our way
through root and tendril, climber
shoot and yellow clinger. This
was the pistil journey in-
to moistened gloom. Dews
dripped, lights twink-
led, crickets chirped and still
the dark was silence, still
the dark was home. We
scorched, we raked, we
settled; cleared path,
cut clearing, burnt the dry rot
out of withered wood to make this farm.
And at night, so that no harm
would come from dark still heavy on us,
made this fire: fire-

flies from sticks, from cinders; and we
sang:

in praise of those who journey
those who find the way

those who clear the path
those who go on before us

to prepare the way.

We sang of warmth and fires,
bodies touching, eyes of embers, watching.

Where are the open spaces now
clear sky, the stars, horizons' distances?

We sang of warmth and fires,
bodies safe and touching.

2

But the lips remember
temples, gods and pharaohs,

gold, silver ware; imagination
rose on wide unfolded wings.

But here in the dark,
we rest;

time to forget
the kings;

time to forget
the gods.

That fat man
with the fire-

light's grease
that dances

on his belly –
belly button

bunged – is he
the king

or glutton?
He lives

on human
blood

and dies
in human

blood;
our empire's

past of stone
and skulls

demands it.
And Ra,

the sun
god's gold,

demanded blood
to make it

sacred.
Time to forget

these kings.
Time to forget

these gods.
The jewelled sun

has splintered
on these leaves.

The moon-
light rusts.

Only the frogs wear jewels
here; the cricket's chirp is

emerald; the praying mantis'
topaz pleases; and termites'

tunnel eyes illuminate the dark.
No sphinx eyes close and dream

us of our destiny; the desert
drifting certainties outside us.

Here leaf eyes shift, twigs
creak, buds flutter, the stick

becomes a snake: uncertainties adrift
within us.

3

But the way lost
is a way to be found
again;

the moist
stones, warm
pebbles of rain,

move into tossed
leaves of darkness; round
my mud hut I hear again

the cry of the lost
swallows, horizons' halloos, found-
ationless voices, voyages . . .

Techiman drizzles in sun-
light; Peki peeps
out of the valley; fun-
loving Nsuta sleeps

in the misty, water-
well'd dawn. Burn
Koforidua, holy tree
blasted by lightning; turn

in your sleep, sleepers
at Krachi; the almond leaves
scratching your rocks, rock
you awake for new journeys; stop-

ping at Golokwati, Kpandu and Pong
for rest, salt and water;
then onward to Teshie,
Labadi, Kaneshie . . .

Time's walking river is long.

The Journeys

I

E-
gypt
in Af-
rica
Mesopo-
tamia
Mero-
ë

the
Nile
silica
glass
and brittle
Sa-
hara, Tim-
buctu, Gao
the hills of
Ahafo, winds
of the Ni-
ger, Kumasi
and Kiver
down the
coiled Congo
and down
that black river
that tides us to hell

Hell
in the water

brown
boys of Bushongo
drowned in the
blue and the bitter
salt of the wave-gullied
Ferdinand's sea
Soft winds
to San Salvador, Christoph-
er, Christ, and no Noah
or dove to promise us, grim
though it was, the simple sal-
vation of love. And so it was Little
Rock, Dall-
as, New Orleans, Santiago
De Cuba, the miles
of unfortunate islands: the

Saints and the Virgins, L'Ouverture's Haiti
ruined by greed and the slow
growing green of its freedom; Golden Guiana:
Potaro
leaping in light liquid amber
in Makonaima's perpetual falls. And as if
the exhaustion of this wasn't all – Egypt,
Meroë, the Congo and all –
in the fall we reached De-
troit, Chicago and Den-
ver; and then it was New
York, selling news-
papers in Brooklyn and Harlem.
Then Capetown and Rio; remember how we
took Paris by storm: Sartre, Camus, Picasso and
    all?
But where are the dreams

of that bug happy, trash-
holstered tropical bed

when Uncle Tom lived
and we cursed him? This
the new deal for we black
grinning jacks? Lights
big like bubbies but we
still in shacks?

2

Tall, with slow
dignity

(so
goes the saying

so
went the dream)

the negro
steps his way among the follies.

With well-cut wood-cut head,
with subtle tie

and fashionably
faun exterieur,

he needs no clowning
to assert himself: no boot

black smile, no warm humility:
no hanging

one-hand from his strength, playing
the black baboon.

He plays his own
game here and plays it

hard: and whether
gentleman or gigolo or

both, he holds himself
aloof from minor glitters

and does not wink
at mouching, long-haired, well-

upholstered fillies, soft in public sweaters,
or turn distracted

head to watch the carefully
arranged and ready nylon

ladies' legs along
the boulevard. His glance

is only for *la femme
exceptionelle*: the leading-

lady with no dissonance
in view: the rich-lipped generous

ewe, returning reconnoitre'd
stare for candid *coup*

d'oeil: the ariadne clue
that tries to trick him, trap him,

track him down and lead him
to himself, the minotaur.

There
he abides: himself: coursing his own

man-
oeuvres: jives calmly, merely nods

his head and keeps
his potent subterranean power

for this his victim lover,
who through the artful

glance
the sacrificial

dance,
delivers him his chance.

Meanwhile he keeps
himself, asking no favours

and expecting
none: taking

his chance
among the dead-

ly follies with this
nonchalance

of shoulder and this
urbane head.

3

So went the black
hatted zoot-
suited watch-
chained dream
of the Panama boys
and the hoods
from Chicago.

Yeah man!
the real ne-
gro, man, real
cool.

Broad back
big you know what
black sperm spews
negritude.

Yeah man!
so went the
mud hut, hole-
hatted glorious

dream. Harlem
was heaven
and Paris a palace
for all.

Yeah man!
and the old man gone
old Uncle Tom gone
rain making souse

of his balls in the soil.
But he's real cool,
man, while we sweat
in this tin trunk'd house

that we rent from the rat
to share with the mouse:

Castries' Conway and Brixton in London,
Port of Spain's jungle

and Kingston's dry Dungle
Chicago Smethwick and Tiger Bay.

4

Never seen
a man
travel more
seen more
lands
than this poor
path-
less harbour-
less spade.

The Twist

In a little shanty town
was on a night like this

girls were sitting down
around the town
like this

some were young
and some were brown
I even found
a miss

who was black and brown
and really did
the twist

watch her move her wrist
and feel your belly twist
feel the hunger thunder
when her hip bones twist

try to hold her, keep her under
while the juke box hiss
twist the music out of hunger
on a night like this.

Wings of a Dove

I

Brother Man the Rasta
man, beard full of lichens
brain full of lice
watched the mice
come up through the floor-
boards of his down-
town, shanty-town kitchen,
and smiled. Blessed are the poor
in health, he mumbled,
that they should inherit this
wealth. Blessed are the meek
hearted, he grumbled,
for theirs is this stealth.

Brother Man the Rasta
man, hair full of lichens
head hot as ice
watched the mice
walk into his poor
hole, reached for his peace
and the pipe of his ganja
and smiled how the mice
eyes, hot pumice
pieces, glowed into his room
like ruby, like rhinestone
and suddenly startled like
diamond.

And I
Rastafar-I

in Babylon's boom
town, crazed by the moon
and the peace of this chalice, I
prophet and singer, scourge
of the gutter, guardian
Trench Town, the Dungle and Young's
Town, rise and walk through the now silent
streets of affliction, hawk's eyes
hard with fear, with
affection, and hear my people
cry, my people
shout:

Down down
white
man, con
man, brown
man, down
down full
man, frown-
ing fat
man, that
white black
man that
lives in
the town.

Rise rise
locks-
man, Solo-
man wise
man, rise
rise rise
leh we
laugh

dem, mock
dem, stop
dem, kill
dem an' go
back back
to the black
man lan'
back back
to Af-
rica.

2

Them doan mean it, yuh know,
them cahn help it
but them clean-face browns in
Babylon town is who I most fear

an' who fears most I.
Watch de vulture dem a-fly-
in', hear de crow a-dem crow:
see what them money a-buy?

Caw caw caw caw.
Ol' crow, ol' crow, cruel ol'
ol' crow, that's all them got
to show.

Crow fly flip flop
hip hop
pun de ground; na
feet feel firm

pun de firm stones; na
good pickney born

from de flesh
o' dem bones;

naw naw naw naw.

3

So beat dem drums
dem, spread

dem wings dem,
watch dem fly

dem, soar dem
high dem,

clear in the glory of the Lord.

Watch dem ship dem
come to town dem

full o' silk dem
full o' food dem

an' dem 'plane dem
come to groun' dem

full o' flash dem
full o' cash dem

silk dem food dem
shoe dem wine dem

that dem drink dem
an' consume dem

praisin' the glory of the Lord.

So beat dem burn
dem, learn

dem that dem
got dem nothin'

but dem
bright bright baubles

that will burst dem
when the flame dem

from on high dem
raze an' roar dem

an' de poor dem
rise an' rage dem

in de glory of the Lord.

Calypso

1

The stone had skidded arc'd and bloomed into islands:
Cuba and San Domingo
Jamaica and Puerto Rico
Grenada Guadeloupe Bonaire

curved stone hissed into reef
wave teeth fanged into clay
white splash flashed into spray
Bathsheba Montego Bay

bloom of the arcing summers . . .

2

The islands roared into green plantations
ruled by silver sugar cane
sweat and profit
cutlass profit
islands ruled by sugar cane

And of course it was a wonderful time
a profitable hospitable well-worth-your-time
when captains carried receipts for rices
letters spices wigs
opera glasses swaggering asses
debtors vices pigs

O it was a wonderful time
an elegant benevolent redolent time –
and young Mrs P's quick irrelevant crime
at four o'clock in the morning . . .

99

3

But what of black Sam
with the big splayed toes
and the shoe black shiny skin?

He carries bucketfuls of water
'cause his Ma's just had another daughter.

And what of John with the European name
who went to school and dreamt of fame
his boss one day called him a fool
and the boss hadn't even been to school ...

4

Steel drum steel drum
hit the hot calypso dancing
hot rum hot rum
who goin' stop this bacchanalling?

For we glance the banjo
dance the limbo
grow our crops by maljo

have loose morals
gather corals
father our neighbour's quarrels

perhaps when they come
with their cameras and straw
hats: sacred pink tourists from the frozen Nawth

we should get down to those
white beaches
where if we don't wear breeches

it becomes an island dance
Some people doin' well
while others are catchin' hell

o the boss gave our Johnny the sack
though we beg him please
please to take 'im back

so the boy now nigratin' overseas . . .

The Emigrants

I

So you have seen them
with their cardboard grips,
felt hats, rain-
cloaks, the women
with their plain
or purple-tinted
coats hiding their fatten-
ed hips.

These are The Emigrants.
On sea-port quays
at air-ports
anywhere where there is ship
or train, swift
motor car, or jet
to travel faster than the breeze
you see them gathered:
passports stamped
their travel papers wrapped
in old disused news-
papers: lining their patient queues.

Where to?
They do not know.
Canada, the Panama
Canal, the Miss-
issippi painfields, Florida?
Or on to dock
at hissing smoke locked
Glasgow?

Why do they go?
They do not know.
Seeking a job
they settle for the very best
the agent has to offer:
jabbing a neighbour
out of work for four bob
less a week.

What do they hope for
what find there
these New World mariners
Columbus coursing kaffirs

What Cathay shores
for them are gleaming golden
what magic keys they carry to unlock
what gold endragoned doors?

2

But now the doors are iron: mouldy
dredges do not care what we discover here:
the Mississippi mud is sticky:

men die there
and bouquets of stench lie
all night long along the river bank.

In London, Undergrounds are cold.
The train rolls in from darkness
with our fears

and leaves a lonely soft metallic clanking
in our ears.
In New York

nights are hot
in Harlem, Brooklyn,
along Long Island Sound

This city is so vast
its ears have ceased to know
a simple human sound

Police cars wail
like babies
an ambulance erupts

like breaking glass
an elevator sighs
like Jews in Europe's gases

then slides us swiftly
down the ropes to hell.
Where is the bell

that used to warn us,
playing cricket on the beach,
that it was mid-day: sun too hot

for heads? And evening's
angelus of fish soup,
prayers, bed?

3

My new boss
has no head
for (female) figures

my lover
has no teeth
does not chew

chicken bones.
Her mother wears
a curly headed wig.

4

Once when we went to Europe, a rich old lady asked:
Have you no language of your own
no way of doing things

did you spend all those holidays
at England's apron strings?

And coming down the Bellevueplatz
a bow-legged workman
said: This country's getting pretty flat
with *negres en Switzerland*.

5

The chaps who drive the City buses
don't like us clipping for them much;
in fact, make quite a fuss.
Bus strikes loom soon.

The men who lever ale
in stuffy Woodbine pubs
don't like us much.
No drinks there soon.

Or broken bottles.
The women who come down
to open doors a crack
will sometimes crack

your fingers if you don't
watch. Sorry!
Full! Not even Bread
and Breakfast soon

for curly headed workers.
So what to do, man?
Ban the Bomb? Bomb
the place down?

Boycott the girls?
Put a ban on all
marriages? Call
You'self X

wear a beard
and a turban
washing your tur-
bulent sex

about six
times a day:
going Muslim?
Black as God

brown is good
white as sin?
An' doan forget Jimmy Baldwin
an' Martin Luther King . . .

6

Our colour beats a restless drum
but only the bitter come.

South

But today I recapture the islands'
bright beaches: blue mist from the ocean
rolling into the fishermen's houses.
By these shores I was born: sound of the sea
came in at my window, life heaved and breathed in me then
with the strength of that turbulent soil.

Since then I have travelled: moved far from the beaches:
sojourned in stoniest cities, walking the lands of the north
in sharp slanting sleet and the hail,
crossed countless savannas and come
to this house in the forest where the shadows oppress me
and the only water is rain and the tepid taste of the river.

We who are born of the ocean can never seek solace
in rivers: their flowing runs on like our longing,
reproves us our lack of endeavour and purpose,
proves that our striving will founder on that.
We resent them this wisdom, this freedom: passing us
toiling, waiting and watching their cunning declension
    down to the sea.

But today I would join you, travelling river,
borne down the years of your patientest flowing,
past pains that would wreck us, sorrows arrest us,
hatred that washes us up on the flats;
and moving on through the plains that receive us,
processioned in tumult, come to the sea.

Bright waves splash up from the rocks to refresh us,
blue sea-shells shift in their wake

and *there* is the thatch of the fishermen's houses, the path
made of pebbles, and look!
Small urchins combing the beaches
look up from their traps to salute us:

they remember us just as we left them.
The fisherman, hawking the surf on this side
of the reef, stands up in his boat
and halloos us: a starfish lies in its pool.
And gulls, white sails slanted seaward,
fly into the limitless morning before us.

Origins

Lips
lips
salt slick of the sea
water

tap of its time on the ground
shore
the pebbles of silence
lap

lap
of my mother
and the eyes of my father
rising

rising
the sea in its splendour
plentiful fishes
crowds, brilliant multitudes of wet

colour
the pool
lying cool in its green
corner

dolour of distances
horizons
sails
fishermen's songs

pails
slop of their catches

the dawn
blinds, open eyes

hands groping for prayer
flowers knowing
the sun-
light

hump-
backs out of the eye
lands, my is-
lands

red clay
mud of volcanoes
bristled with jewels
rot of word

stone, water's opposition
your lips
face on my face
cheek to my stone

sheet, green
energies, cuts
rivers, delicate
fingers, tongs

of a sound, sudden blue flowings
the street's avalanche of bicycle bells
claxons, screams,
flags over Kingston . . .

The piston
engine dreams

of a kerosene god; hell
here is a black wick without whisper

of flame; red flowerings
of horsemen rise into chrysanthemum heat; the young
know no older love than a fat bottomed dissolute sister;
    the plates
in the kitchen are cracked into green, ganjarene. Rut

rut rut me you pig of pain, you
mean anger, tapper of marrow, bone
snapper; your face is my face,
your lips suckle my parasites. Sit

still you bisexual cycler: passion
of the bread broken, the east rising in its blood.
What prayers will assuage these jewels
my eyes, the laid-out islands, roses

stripped naked in the dew? What prayers
will reprieve the cold fever of the day-
light, thin man, knocking at doors, smile
sharpened by the rats, tin can

of pisstilence, scruffulent scrubber,
saviour of the harbour's sepulchres of filth.
Lock me dead in your eye
as the cock crows: red rain of urine falls slowly on the is-

lands; the dump-
heaps sprout pain again: guerr-
illas of green duck-
ing under the twisted barb wired night

and the sun
cunning
cannon of flowers, swaying
swaying: sip sop, sweet sop, sour sapodilla's eyes

the eyes of the prawns
in the basket, tickless in death, water's wristwatch;
the wails
coming up from the gullies

frog songs
and the mouth organ drool of the snails'
slow passage, discretion, through zones
that the hummingbird's swiftness

that is stillness, knows not, knows not;
and the lourd
hedgehog, following the mongoose and the mangrove
trail, reaches the green
pool

lured
by the birth pangs of bubbles
the silt slow wet
of the mosquito's malarial reaches

Till the sun enters fine, enters fine, enters fin-
ally its growing circle of splendour
rising
rising

into the eyes of my father
the fat valley loads of my mother
of water, lapp-
ing, lapping my ankles, lapp-

ing these shores with their silence:
insistence of pure
light, pure pouring of water
that opens the eyes of my window

and I see you, my wound-
ed gift giver of sea
spoken syllables: words salt on your lips
on my lips . . .

Tom

Under the burnt out green
of this small yard's
tufts of grass
where water was once used
to wash pots, pans, poes,
ochre appears. A rusted
bucket, hole kicked into its
bottom, lies on its side.

Fence, low wall of careful
stones marking the square
yard, is broken now, breached
by pigs, by rats, by mongoose
and by neighbours. Eucalyptus
bushes push their way amidst
the marl. All looks so left
so unlived in: yard, fence and cabin.

Here old Tom lived: his whole
tight house no bigger than your
sitting room. Here was his world
banged like a fist on broken
chairs, bare table and the side-
board dresser where he kept his cups.
One wooden only door, still latched,
hasp broken; one window, wooden,
broken; four slats still intact.
Darkness pours from these wrecked boards
and from the crab torn spaces underneath the door.

These are the deepest reaches of time's long
attack. The roof, dark shingles,

silvered in some places by the wind, the finger-
tips of weather, shines still secure, still
perfect, although the plaster peels from walls,
at sides, at back, from high up near the roof: in places
where it was not painted. But from the front,
the face from which it looked out on the world,
the house retains its lemon wash as smooth and bland as
    pearl.

But the tide creeps in: today's
insistence laps the loneliness of this
resisting cabin: the village grows and bulges:
shops, super-
market, Postal Agency
whose steel-spectacled mistress
rules the town. But no one knows
where Tom's cracked limestone oblong lies.
The house, the Postal Agent says,
is soon to be demolished:
a Housing Estate's being spawned
to feed the greedy town.

No one
knows Tom now, no one cares.
Slave's days are past, for-
gotten. The faith, the dream denied,
the things he dared
not do, all lost, if un-
forgiven. This house is all
that's left of hopes, of hurt,
of history . . .

The Leopard

1

Caught therefore in this care-
ful cage of glint, rock,

water ringing the island's
doubt, his

terror dares
not blink. A nervous tick-

like itch picks
at the corners of his

lips. The lean flanks quick
and quiver until the

tension cracks his
ribs. If he could only

strike or trigger
off his fury. But cunning

cold bars break his
rage; and stretched to strike,

his stretched claws strike
no glory.

2

There was a land not long
ago where it was other-
wise; where he was happy.

That fatal plunge down from the
tree on antelope or duiker,
was freedom for him then.

But somewhere in the dampened
dark, the marks –
man watched, the strings were

stretched, the tricky traps were
ready. Yet had he felt
his supple force would fall

to such confinement,
would he, to dodge his doom
and guarantee his movement,

have paused from stalking deer
or striking down the duiker;
or would he, face to fate,

have merely murdered more?

3

But he must do
what fate had forced him to.

At birth his blood
was bent upon a flood

that forged him forward
on its deadly springs.

His paws grew heavy
and his claws shone sharp.

Unleashed, his passion
slashed and mangled with its stainless

steel. No flesh he raped
would ever heal. Like grape

crushed in the mouth, to you,
was each new death to him.

Each death he dealt perfected him.
His victims felt this single

soft intention in him; as gentle
as a pigeon winging home.

4

Now he stands caged.
The monkeys lisp and leer
and rip and hammer
at their barriers.

He burns and paces,
turns again and paces,
disdaining admiration in those faces
that peep and pander at him

through the barriers.
Give him a tree to leap from,
liberator. In pity let him
once more move with his soft

spotted and untroubled splendour
among the thrills and whispers
of his glinting kingdom.
Or unlock him and now let him

from this triggered branch
and guillotining vantage,
in one fine final falling
fall upon the quick fear-

footed deer or peer-
less antelope whose beauty,
ravaged by his sharp brutality,
propitiates the ancient guilt

each feels toward the other:
the victim's wish to hurt;
the hunter's not to.
But by this sacrifice

of strong to helpless other,
healed and aneled:
both hurt and hunter
by this fatal lunge made whole.

5

Yet he chose otherwise.
Foolish or wise,
to be a beast

like you, like me,
this was the least
he wanted. Force

fashions force;
master makes over—
mastering slave

and cruelty breeds
a litter of bright
evils.

So he chose otherwise.
Foolish or wise,
his hand upon his

hatred's anvil,
he did not strike
the white

slave master down;
the promptings of his
tragic hammer

held him dumb;
the forge
throbbed fury

yet he let the fear-
ful flare cool down;
the eyes stared

outward from the future
of heroic bronze: suc-
cessful insurrections,

busha's fall . . .
metal was melted,
mould was made,

the sterling ring-
ing ready;
he only

had to hit,
to hold the hammer
steady.

But as the hammer-
head swung up
and upward, bright

with blows, he
paused; poised
in that fatal attitude

that would have smashed
the world, or made it, he
let the hammer

down; made
nothing, un-
made nothing;

his bright
hopes down,
his own

slight failure
dumb,
his one

heroic flare
and failure
done.

6

So silent in its care-
ful cage

his terror dares
not blink.

Light fades,
you leave

these lonely places
to the watchman and his

dog. Behind you
locks click

shut, wheels
turn, and rain

obscures the view.
His terror, caged, still

paces, turns
again and

paces. Time
ticks

still.
Which one

of you
with doubt—

ing, fearing faces,
will return

to where this
future paces

and dare
to let it out.

EDWIN MORGAN

After The Party

Did you touch me? I thought
at the door, as the party broke up violently,
streaming out into dark snow –
who wants to remember the bad wine,
the worse coffee, that raving blond on the stair
with his jagged half of a Mingus E P dipped in punch–
or his friend old whimpering cut-wrist
squirming on his paunch on the bathroom carpet/imagine
a white fitted carpet and a botched suicide, but the host
went on smiling as he shooed us into the cold. The old
lizard clutched his dressing-gown about him though – I
    know.
I sat on the step and rolled myself a cigarette,
I remember that. It was just before,
in that struggle in the doorway,
all coats and hiccups and fumbling, that I thought
you touched me. I know you were sober
and I was mostly. You never looked at me
but you touched me. Didn't you?
It's all I want to remember
and yet it becomes less clear
than that crazy slut sobbing through the banisters.
What could you get from it? My doubt is
that you even remember it. Or are you waiting
for me to find you? And what would happen then?

It all slips through my hands like snow in silence.

Brush me with your wing,
I'm lying here
in my shadows, the ones
for that night's sake.

To Joan Eardley

Pale yellow letters
humbly straggling across
the once brilliant red
of a broken shop-face
CONFECTIO
and a blur of children
at their games, passing,
gazing as they pass
at the blur of sweets
in the dingy, cosy
Rottenrow window –
an Eardley on my wall.
Such rags and streaks
that master us ! –
that fix what the pick
and bulldozer have crumbled
to a dingier dust,
the living blur
fiercely guarding
energy that has vanished,
cries filling still
the unechoing close !
I wandered by the rubble
and the houses left standing
kept a chill, dying life
in their islands of stone.
No window opened
as the coal cart rolled
and the coalman's call
fell coldly to the ground.
But the shrill children
jump on my wall.

King Billy

Grey over Riddrie the clouds piled up,
dragged their rain through the cemetery trees.
The gates shone cold. Wind rose
flaring the hissing leaves, the branches
swung, heavy, across the lamps.
Gravestones huddled in drizzling shadow,
flickering streetlight scanned the requiescats,
a name and an urn, a date, a dove
picked out, lost, half regained.
What is this dripping wreath, blown from its grave
red, white, blue, and gold
'To Our Leader of Thirty Years Ago'

Bareheaded, in dark suits, with flutes
and drums, they brought him here, in procession
seriously, King Billy of Bridgeton, dead,
from Bridgeton Cross: a memory of violence,
brooding days of empty bellies,
billiard smoke and a sour pint,
boots or fists, famous sherrickings,
the word, the scuffle, the flash, the shout,
bloody crumpling in the close,
bricks for papish windows, get
the Conks next time, the Conks ambush
the Billy Boys, the Billy Boys the Conks till
Sillitoe scuffs the razors down the stank –
No, but it isn't the violence they remember
but the legend of a violent man
born poor, gang-leader in the bad times
of idleness and boredom, lost in better days,
a bouncer in a betting club,

a quiet man at last, dying
alone in Bridgeton in a box bed.
So a thousand people stopped the traffic
for the hearse of a folk hero and the flutes
threw 'Onward Christian Soldiers' to the winds
from unironic lips, the mourners kept
in step, and there were some who wept.

Go from the grave. The shrill flutes
are silent, the march dispersed.
Deplore what is to be deplored,
and then find out the rest.

The Suspect

Asked me for a match suddenly / with his hand up
I thought he was after my wallet
gave him a shove / he fell down
dead on the pavement at my feet
he was forty-two, a respectable man they said
anyone can have a bad heart I told the police
but they've held me five hours and don't
tell me the innocent don't feel
guilty in the glaring chair

I didn't kill you / I didn't know you
I did push you / I did fear you
accusing me from the mortuary drawer
like a damned white ghost I don't believe in
– then why were you afraid / are you used to attacks
by men who want a match / what sort
of life you lead / you were bloody quick
with your hands when you pushed him
what did you think he was and do you think
we don't know what you are / take it
all down / the sweat of the innocent by god we'll see
and not by the hundred-watt bulb of the anglepoise either
give him a clip on the ear jack / you
bastard in your shroud if I feared you then
I hate you now you
no I don't you poor dead man I put you there
I don't I don't
but just

if you could get up / to speak for me
I am on trial / do you understand

I am not guilty / whatever the light says
whatever the sweat says
/ they've noticed my old scar
to be killed by a dead man is no fight
they're starting again
so / your story is he asked you for a light
– yes suddenly / and put his hand up / I thought
he was after my wallet, gave him
a shove, he fell as I told you
dead, it was his heart,
at my feet, as I said

Trio

Coming up Buchanan Street, quickly, on a sharp winter
  evening
a young man and two girls, under the Christmas lights –
The young man carries a new guitar in his arms,
the girl on the inside carries a very young baby,
and the girl on the outside carries a chihuahua.
And the three of them are laughing, their breath rises
in a cloud of happiness, and as they pass
the boy says, 'Wait till he sees this but!'
The chihuahua has a tiny Royal Stewart tartan coat like a
  teapot-holder,
the baby in its white shawl is all bright eyes and mouth like
  favours in a fresh sweet cake,
the guitar swells out under its milky plastic cover, tied at
  the neck with silver tinsel tape and a brisk sprig of
  mistletoe.
Orphean sprig! Melting baby! Warm chihuahua!
The vale of tears is powerless before you.
Whether Christ is born, or is not born, you
put paid to fate, it abdicates
                              under the Christmas lights.
Monsters of the year
go blank, are scattered back,
can't bear this march of three.

– And the three have passed, vanished in the crowd
(yet not vanished, for in their arms they wind
the life of men and beasts, and music,
laughter ringing them round like a guard)
at the end of this winter's day.

Good Friday

Three o'clock. The bus lurches
round into the sun. 'D's this go – '
he flops beside me – 'right along Bath Street?
– Oh tha's, tha's all right, see I've
got to get some Easter eggs for the kiddies.
I've had a wee drink, ye understand –
ye'll maybe think it's a – funny day
to be celebrating – well, no, but ye see
I wasny working, and I like to celebrate
when I'm no working – I don't say it's right
I'm no saying it's right, ye understand – ye understand?
But anyway tha's the way I look at it –
I'm no boring you, eh? – ye see today,
take today, I don't know what today's in aid of,
whether Christ was – crucified or was he –
rose fae the dead like, see what I mean?
You're an educatit man, you can tell me –
– Aye, well. There ye are. It's been seen
time and again, the working man
has nae education, he jist canny – jist
hasny got it, know what I mean,
he's jist bliddy ignorant – Christ aye,
bliddy ignorant. Well – ' The bus brakes violently,
he lunges for the stair, swings down – off,
into the sun for his Easter eggs,
on very
            nearly
                    steady
                            legs.

In The Snack-Bar

A cup capsizes along the formica,
slithering with a dull clatter.
A few heads turn in the crowded evening snack-bar.
An old man is trying to get to his feet
from the low round stool fixed to the floor.
Slowly he levers himself up, his hands have no power.
He is up as far as he can get. The dismal hump
looming over him forces his head down.
He stands in his stained beltless gaberdine
like a monstrous animal caught in a tent
in some story. He sways slightly,
the face not seen, bent down
in shadow under his cap.
Even on his feet he is staring at the floor
or would be, if he could see.
I notice now his stick, once painted white
but scuffed and muddy, hanging from his right arm.
Long blind, hunchback born, half paralysed
he stands
fumbling with the stick
and speaks:
'I want – to go to the – toilet.'

It is down two flights of stairs, but we go.
I take his arm. 'Give me – your arm – it's better,' he says.
Inch by inch we drift towards the stairs.
A few yards of floor are like a landscape
to be negotiated, in the slow setting out
time has almost stopped. I concentrate
my life to his: crunch of spilt sugar,
slidy puddle from the night's umbrellas,

table edges, people's feet,
hiss of the coffee-machine, voices and laughter,
smell of a cigar, hamburgers, wet coats steaming,
and the slow dangerous inches to the stairs.
I put his right hand on the rail
and take his stick. He clings to me. The stick
is in his left hand, probing the treads.
I guide his arm and tell him the steps.
And slowly we go down. And slowly we go down.
White tiles and mirrors at last. He shambles
uncouth into the clinical gleam.
I set him in position, stand behind him
and wait with his stick.
His brooding reflection darkens the mirror
but the trickle of his water is thin and slow,
an old man's apology for living.
Painful ages to close his trousers and coat —
I do up the last buttons for him.
He asks doubtfully, 'Can I — wash my hands?'
I fill the basin, clasp his soft fingers round the soap.
He washes, feebly, patiently. There is no towel.
I press the pedal of the drier, draw his hands
gently into the roar of the hot air.
But he cannot rub them together,
drags out a handkerchief to finish.
He is glad to leave the contraption, and face the stairs.
He climbs, and steadily enough.
He climbs, we climb. He climbs
with many pauses but with that one
persisting patience of the undefeated
which is the nature of man when all is said.
And slowly we go up. And slowly we go up.
The faltering, unfaltering steps
take him at last to the door

across that endless, yet not endless waste of floor.
I watch him helped on a bus. It shudders off in the rain.
The conductor bends to hear where he wants to go.

Wherever he could go it would be dark
and yet he must trust men.
Without embarrassment or shame
he must announce his most pitiful needs
in a public place. No one sees his face.
Does he know how frightening he is in his strangeness
under his mountainous coat, his hands like wet leaves
stuck to the half-white stick?
His life depends on many who would evade him.
But he cannot reckon up the chances,
having one thing to do,
to haul his blind hump through these rains of August.
Dear Christ, to be born for this!

Glasgow Green

Clammy midnight, moonless mist.
A cigarette glows and fades on a cough.
Meth-men mutter on benches, pawed
by river fog. Monteith Row
sweats coldly, crumbles, dies
slowly. All shadows are alive.
Somewhere a shout's forced out – 'No!' –
it leads to nothing but silence,
except the whisper of the grass
and the other whispers that fill the shadows.

'What d'ye mean see me again?
D'ye think I came here jist for that?
I'm no finished with you yet.
I can get the boys t'ye, they're no that faur away.
You wouldny like that eh? Look there's no two ways aboot
   it.
Christ but I'm gaun to have you Mac
if it takes all night, turn over you bastard
turn over, I'll – '
                Cut the scene.
Here there's no crying for help,
it must be acted out, again, again.
This is not the delicate nightmare
you carry to the point of fear
and wake from, it is life, the sweat
is real, the wrestling under a bush
is real, the dirty starless river
is the real Clyde, with a dishrag dawn
it rinses the horrors of the night
but cannot make them clean,

though washing blows
                    where the women watch
by day,
        and children run,
                        on Glasgow Green.

And how shall these men live?
Providence, watch them go!
Watch them love, and watch them die!
How shall the race be served?
It shall be served by anguish
as well as by children at play.
It shall be served by loneliness
as well as by family love.
It shall be served by hunter and hunted in their endless
    chain
as well as by those who turn back the sheets in peace.
The thorn in the flesh!
Providence, water it!
Do you think it is not watered?
Do you think it is not planted?
Do you think there is not a seed of the thorn
as there is also a harvest of the thorn?
Man, take in that harvest!
Help that tree to bear its fruit!
Water the wilderness, walk there, reclaim it!
Reclaim, regain, renew! Fill the barns and the vats!

Longing,
        longing
                shall find its wine.

Let the women sit in the Green
and rock their prams as the sheets

blow and whip in the sunlight.
But the beds of married love
are islands in a sea of desire.
Its waves break here, in this park,
splashing the flesh as it trembles
like driftwood through the dark.

Phoning

The roofs and cranes
and the dark rain

I look back
remembering an evening
we sat on the bed
and I dialled Montreux
a sudden impulse
we had to laugh
at that chain of numbers
0104121615115
Grand Hôtel des Alpes
and we spoke to your sister
Glasgow to the snows
and the sunny funiculars
and meetings by a lake
so far from Law and
the pits and cones
of worked Lanarkshire
my arm on your shoulder
held you as you spoke
your voice vibrating
as you leaned against me
remembering this
and your finger tapping
my bare knee
to emphasize a point
but most of all
in that dusky room
the back of your head
as you bent to catch

the distant words
caught my heart
vulnerable
as the love
with which I make
this sunset chain
remembering

deep in the city
far from the snows

Drift

Rhododendron dust rose
and fell in the June wind –
lightness, lightness!
And with an arm I
swept the loch away
from your eyes. Drowsy
picnic-fires, the cars,
the wood-pigeon, the spray
of water-skiers through the trees
went fading tangled
off the world.
Only stars of heat
pricked, and your cigarette
smouldered in the grass
forgotten, its blue pungence
not to be forgotten
blown across our faces
with the rhododendron-drift.
Love, pillow me
by the eastern tree.

An Addition To The Family: for M.L.

A musical poet, collector of basset-horns,
was buttering his toast down in Dunbartonshire
when suddenly from behind the breakfast newspaper
the shining blade stopped scraping
and he cried to his wife, 'Joyce, listen to this! –
"Two basset-hounds for sale, house-trained, keen
  hunters" –
Oh we must have them! What d'you think?' 'But dear,
did you say *hounds*?' Yes yes, hounds, hounds –'
'But Maurice, it's *horns* we want, you must be over
in the livestock column, you can't play a hound!'
'It's Beverley it says, the kennels are at Beverley –'
'But Maurice –' ' ' – I'll get some petrol, we'll be there by
  lunchtime –'
'But a dog, two dogs, where'll we put them?'
'I've often wondered what these dogs are like –'
'You mean you don't even –' 'Is there no more
  marmalade?'
' – don't know what they look like? And how are we to
  feed them?
Yes, there's the pot dear.' 'This stuff's all peel, isn't it?'
'Well, we're at the end of it. But look, these two great –'
'You used to make marmalade once upon a time.'
'They've got ears down to here, and they're far too –'
'Is that half past eight? I'll get the car out.
See if I left my cheque-book on the –' 'Maurice,
are you mad? What about your horns?' 'What horns,
what are you talking about? Look Joyce dear,
if it's not on the dresser it's in my other jacket.
I believe they're wonderful for rabbits –'

So the musical poet took his car to Beverley
with his wife and his cheque-book, and came back home
with his wife and his cheque-book and two new hostages
to the unexpectedness of fortune.
The creatures scampered through the grass, the children
came out with cries of joy, there seemed to be nothing
dead or dying in all that landscape.
Fortune bless the unexpected cries!
Life gathers to the point of wishing it,
a mocking pearl of many ventures. The house
rolled on its back and kicked its legs in the air.
And later, wondering farmers as they passed would hear
behind the lighted window in the autumn evening
two handsome mellow-bosomed basset-hounds
howling to a melodious basset-horn.

Aberdeen Train

Rubbing a glistening circle
on the steamed-up window I framed
a pheasant in a field of mist.
The sun was a great red thing somewhere low,
struggling with the milky scene. In the furrows
a piece of glass winked into life,
hypnotized the silly dandy; we
hooted past him with his head cocked,
contemplating a bottle-end.
And this was the last of October,
a Chinese moment in the Mearns.

The Flowers Of Scotland

Yes, it is too cold in Scotland for flower people; in any case
  who would be handed a thistle?
What are our flowers? Locked swings and private rivers –
and the island of Staffa for sale in the open market, which no
  one questions or thinks strange –
and lads o' pairts that run to London and Buffalo without a
  backward look while their elders say Who'd blame them –
and bonny fechters kneedeep in dead ducks with all the
  thrawn intentness of the incorrigible professional Scot –
and a Kirk Assembly that excels itself in the bad old
  rhetoric and tries to stamp out every glow of charity and
  change, most wrong when it thinks most loudly it is
  most right –
and a Scottish National Party that refuses to discuss
  Vietnam and is even applauded for doing so, do they
  think no lesson is to be learned from what is going on
  there? –
and the unholy power of Grouse-moor and Broad-acres to
  prevent the smoke of useful industry from sullying
  Invergordon or setting up linear cities among the
  whaups –
and the banning of Beardsley and Joyce but not of course
  of 'Monster on the Campus' or 'Curse of the Undead' –
  those who think the former are the more degrading,
  what are their values? –
and the steady creep of the preservationist societies,
  wearing their pens out for slums with good leaded
  lights – if they could buy all the amber in the Baltic and
  melt it over Edinburgh would they be happy then? – the
  skeleton is well-proportioned –
and by contrast the massive indifference to the slow death

of the Clyde estuary, decline of resorts, loss of steamers,
anaemia of yachting, cancer of monstrous installations of
a foreign power and an acquiescent government – what
is the smell of death on a child's spade, any more than
rats to leaded lights? –
and dissidence crying in the wilderness to a moor of
boulders and two ospreys –
these are the flowers of Scotland.

Archives

generation upon
generation upon
generation upon
generation upon
generation upon
generation upon
generation upon
generation upon
generation upon
generation upon
generation upon
generation upon
generation upon
generation upon
generation upon
generation upon
generation upon
generation upon
generation upon
g neration upon
g neration up n
g nerat on up n
g nerat n up n
g nerat n p n
g erat n p n
g era   n p n
g era   n   n
g er   n   n
g   r   n   n
g   n   n
g   n
g

Che

Even after the body
had been roughly brought
down to Vallegrande
from the hills, and the eyes
had that meaningless glaze
staring at no world,
eyes took meaning from
his slightly parted lips
showing the teeth
in a smile – no rage,
no throes, nothing
but that uncanny pro-
jection of consciousness
and a dead man putting
fate in bondage
to him. Bolivia:
what other bondages
will shiver in the cane-break
even in steel, and will break,
uniforms and proclamations
ploughed under by the very grass
itself – it rises
into the voices of forests.
For the dead wander
among its deep roots
like water, and push
the green land into heroes.
They grow in understanding,
tree, tree, man, man,
move like shadows.
Blossoms brushed

by silent bandoliers
spring out in shock and
back into place.
But jungles break.

Down from the mountains
miles and miles
a marble face,
a broken body.
The marble is only
broken by a smile.

The Old Man and the Sea

And a white mist rolled out of the Pacific
and crept over the sand, stirring nothing –
cold, cold as nothing is cold
on those living highways, moved in
over the early morning trucks,
chilling the drivers in their cabins
(one stops for a paper cup
of coffee, stares out through the steam
at the mist, his hands on the warm cup
imagine the coldness, he throws out the cup
and swears as the fog rolls in, drives on
frowning to feel its touch on his face) –
and seagulls came to shriek at cockcrow
swooping through the wakening farms,
and the smoke struggled from the lumber camps
up into the smoke from the sea,
hovered in the sunless morning
as a lumberman whistled at the pump,
and sea-mist took the flash from the axe.
And above the still lakes of Oregon
and the Blue Mountains into Idaho
eastward, white wings brushing the forests,
a white finger probing the canyon
by Wood River, delicate, persistent, at last
finding by the half-light, in a house of stone,
a white-bearded man like an old sea-captain
cleaning a gun. – Keep back the sea,
keep back the sea! No reassurance
in that daybreak with no sun,
his blood thin, flesh patched and scarred,
eyes grown weary of hunting

and the great game all uncaught.
It was too late to fight the sea.
The raised barrel hardly gleamed
in that American valley, the shot
insulted the morning, crude and quick
with the end of a great writer's life –
fumbling nothing, but leaving questions
that echo beyond Spain and Africa.
Questions, not answers, chill the heart here,
a chained dog whining in the straw,
the gunsmoke marrying the sea-mist,
and silence of the inhuman valleys.

The Death of Marilyn Monroe

What innocence? Whose guilt? What eyes? Whose breast?
Crumpled orphan, nembutal bed,
white hearse, Los Angeles,
DiMaggio! Los Angeles! Miller! Los Angeles! America!
That Death should seem the only protector —
That all arms should have faded, and the great cameras and
    lights become an inquisition and a torment —
That the many acquaintances, the autograph-hunters, the
    inflexible directors, the drive-in admirers should become
    a blur of incomprehension and pain —
That lonely Uncertainty should limp up, grinning, with
    bewildering barbiturates, and watch her undress and lie
    down and in her anguish
call for him! call for him to strengthen her with what
    could only dissolve her! A method
of dying, we are shaken, we see it. Strasberg!
Los Angeles! Olivier! Los Angeles! Others die
and yet by this death we are a little shaken, we feel it,
America.
Let no one say communication is a cantword.
They had to lift her hand from the bedside telephone.
But what she had not been able to say
perhaps she had said. 'All I had was my life.
I have no regrets, because if I made
any mistakes, I was responsible.
There is now — and there is the future.
What has happened is behind. So
it follows you around? So what?' — This
to a friend, ten days before.
And so she was responsible.
And if she was not responsible, not wholly responsible,

Los Angeles? Los Angeles? Will it follow you around?
Will the slow white hearse of the child of America
follow you around?

Astrodome

As real grass withers in the Astrodome [at Houston, Texas]
it has been replaced by Astrograss.

(news item)

all is not grass that astrograss
that astrograss is not all grass
that grass is not all astrograss
astrograss is not all that grass
is that astrograss not all glass
not all astrograss is that glass
all that glass is not astrograss
that is not all astrograss glass
that glass is not all fibreglass
not all that fibreglass is glass
fibreglass is not all that glass
is that not all fibreglass glass
that fibreglass is not all grass
glass is not all that fibreglass
is all astrograss not that glass
all is not grass that fibreglass

Not Playing the Game

– Although a poem is
undoubtedly a 'game'
it is not a game.
And although now it is even
part of the game to say so,
making it a ' " "game" " '
is spooky, and we'll
not play that.

– Who are you kidding, said
the next card. You just played.

– Anything I play
has no rules, if
you see the rules
it's only 'play' –
the 'dealer's eyeshade'.

– I like that smoker's cough the ' " "dealer's eyeshade" ' ".
Your deal is showing, my dear.

– Back in the box you go in words.
'Back in the box', in other words.
Now we'll just let that
' " ' "dealer's eyeshade" ' " '
wilt on whatever can support it, like
a poem on baize.

A Snib for the Nones

Who ever starved in solitary?
There's water, darkness, bread, silence, air.
What is this story of 'No pity'!
Does taking silk involve speaking silk,
acting silk, with a moiré mercy
running at every shot from justice?

You can't read bibles, grow roses there?
What is this extraordinary
exclamatory 'Calamity'!
You've no Harry James, no Henry James,
no matadors and no Matterhorn?
No matter; what sang when you were born!

It is the unquerulous in the
discipline who appear born again.
They fed on patience in darkness or
on darkness in patience; on the bread
of silence, on the bread of silence
deep in the battery of justice.

A Courtly Overture

Most wintry reel,
my frozen court,
hoarfrosted floor
of the gay, my flora,
my pick of dancers,
dancers of my humour,
humour of ice,
till the viols are still
dance with me, dance.

Sway on so,
dancer of glass
in the arms of glass,
mad but no nearer,
cold in unchastity
still. The violcry
lashes the crystal
of your back as it turns
and gleams turning
in these arms of ice.
Dance with me, dance.

Stark the orchestra,
steely the strings,
distant the castanet
in a dark hand,
darkest the hands
that trouble the troubler
the drum. Coast,
dancers, with skill
the drumberg boom.

Glass are the ships,
the fools are glass.
If fools on this floor
spacious and specious
gamble foundering
in musical hurricanes
dance with me, dance —

on into silence,
Gaveston, silence,
Gaveston, Gaveston.
(I hear in the wake
the wail of viols
when we die to the storm
and away from the fools
sway in our harmony
harbourward to calm.)
Flash in these courts, and
glide from these ports, and
dance with me, dance.

The White Rhinoceros

Rare over most of its former range.
                    (*Webster's Third New International Dictionary*)

The white rhinoceros was eating phosphorus!
I came up and I shouted Oh no! No! No! –
you'll be extinct in two years! But he shook his ears
and went on snorting, knee-deep in pawpaws,
trundling his hunger, shrugged off the tick-birds,
rolled up his sleeves, kicked over an anthill,
crunched, munched, wonderful windfall,
empty dish. And gored that old beat-up tin tray
for more, it stuck on his horn,
looked up with weird crown on his horn
like a bear with a beehive, began to glow –
as leerie lair bear glows honeybrown –
but he glowed
                    white and
                                        bright and
the safety-catches started to click in the thickets
for more. Run, holy hide – take up your armour –
run – white horn, tin clown, crown of rain-woods,
venerable shiner! Run, run, run!

And thunders glowing like a phantom
through the bush, beating the guns
this time, but will he always
when his only camouflage
is a world of white?

Save the vulnerable shiners.
Watch the phosphorus trappers.
Smash the poisonous dish.

Frontier Story

Meanwhile, back at the ranch factory
they were turning out whole stampedes
just for the hell of it, the mile-long door slid back
and they reverted to dust at the first touch of air.
But the music of the dust flowed back over the assembly-line
and that was the Christmas of a thousand million cowboys.

Steers went lowing upland, purple sage country
with boots on marched west out back as
bulldozers like mobile capital cities
trunched up dead million-bed motels and charged
some gaily eroded buttes with simulating cowboys.

The diggers were worse than any sands of the sea
and dynamite only loosened myriads off sideways
till a bag of megatons went critical and
there were horses' eyeholes all over the Coalsack
and when we came in we were crunching through cowboys.

Or so we were told as we laid Los Angeles on Boston
and took a few states out, we were only playing,
pulled Mexico up over us and went to sleep,
woke up spitting out Phoenicians into the Cassiterides
and gave a yawn a wave as it flew out full of cowboys.

They sat in our teeth with red-hot spurs and I said
'Back to the drawing-board', but the belt was humming
and pushed the continuum into funky gopher-holes
with a prime number down each hole wheezing
so cheekily we had to make more cowboys

first. Meanwhile, back at the ranch
factory they were diligently making
us, just for the hell of it, the mile-long door
slid back and we reverted to dust at the touch
of air. But our music lingers in the bones of cowboys.

The Computer's First Christmas Card

jollymerry
hollyberry
jollyberry
merryholly
happyjolly
jollyjelly
jellybelly
bellymerry
hollyheppy
jollyMolly
marryJerry
merryHarry
hoppyBarry
heppyJarry
boppyheppy
berryjorry
jorryjolly
moppyjelly
Mollymerry
Jerryjolly
bellyboppy
jorryhoppy
hollymoppy
Barrymerry
Jarryhappy
happyboppy
boppyjolly
jollymerry
merrymerry
merrymerry
merryChris

EDWIN MORGAN

a mmerryasa
Chrismerry
as MERRYCHR
YSANTHEMUM

A View of Things

what I love about dormice is their size
what I hate about rain is its sneer
what I love about the Bratach Gorm is its unflappability
what I hate about scent is its smell
what I love about newspapers is their etaoin shrdl
what I hate about philosophy is its pursed lip
what I love about Rory is his old grouse
what I hate about Pam is her pinkie
what I love about semi-precious stones is their
    preciousness
what I hate about diamonds is their mink
what I love about poetry is its ion engine
what I hate about hogs is their setae
what I love about love is its porridge-spoon
what I hate about hate is its eyes
what I love about hate is its salts
what I hate about love is its dog
what I love about Hank is his string vest
what I hate about the twins is their three gloves
what I love about Mabel is her teeter
what I hate about gooseberries is their look, feel, smell, and
    taste
what I love about the world is its shape
what I hate about a gun is its lock, stock, and barrel
what I love about bacon-and-eggs is its predictability
what I hate about derelict buildings is their reluctance to
    disintegrate
what I love about a cloud is its unpredictability
what I hate about you, chum, is your china
what I love about many waters is their inability to quench
    love

In Sobieski's Shield

well the prophets were dancing in the end much
good it did them and the sun didn't rise at all
anywhere but we weren't among the frozen we had been
dematerialized the day before solar withdrawal
in a hurry it's true but by the best technique
who said only technique well anyhow the best
available and here we are now rematerialized
to the best of my knowledge on a minor planet
of a sun in Sobieski's Shield in our right mind I hope
approximately though not unshaken and admittedly
not precisely those who set out if one can
speak of it by that wellworn tellurian euphemism
in any case molecular reconstitution is no
sinecure even with mice and I wouldn't have been
utterly surprised if some of us had turned out
mice or worse

but at least not that or not yet the effects
of violent change are still slightly present an
indescribable stringent sensation like perhaps being
born or dying but no neither of these I am
very nearly who I was I see I have only
four fingers on my left hand and there's a sharp
twinge I never had in my knee and one most curious
I almost said birthmark and so it is in a sense
light brown shaped like a crazy heart spreading
across my right forearm well let it be we are
here my wife my son the rest of the laboratory
my wife has those streaks of fiery red in her
hair that is expected in women she looks very
frightened yet and lies rigid the rematerialization

is slow in her but that is probably better yes
her eyes flutter to mine questioning I nod can I
smile I think I can does she see me yes thank god
she is hardly altered apart from that extraordinarily
strange and beautiful crown of bright red hair
I draw her head into my arms and hide the sobbing
shuddering first breaths of her second life I don't
know what made me use that phrase who are we
if we are not who we were we have only
one life though we are huddled now in our
protective dome on this harsh metallic plain
that belches cobalt from its craters under a
white-bronze pulsing gong of a sun it was all
they could do for us light-years away it seemed suitable
dematerialization's impossible over short distances anyway
so let's start moving I can surely get onto my feet
yes hoy there

my son is staring fascinated at my four fingers
you've only one nipple I tell him and it's true
but for compensation when he speaks his boy's
treble has broken and at thirteen he is a man
what a limbo to lose childhood in where has
it gone between the throwing of a switch and these
alien iron hills across so many stars his blue eyes
are the same but there's a new graveness of the
second life that phrase again we go up together
to the concave of the dome the environment after all
has to be studied

is that a lake of mercury I can't quite see
through the smoke of the fumarole it's lifting now
but there's something puzzling even when I
my memory of mercury seems to be confused with

what is it blood no no mercury's not like blood
what then what is it I'm remembering or nearly
remembering look dad mercury he says and so it
must be but I see a shell-hole filled with rain-water
red in the sinking sun I know that landscape too
one of the wars far back twentieth century I think the
great war was it called France Flanders fields I remember
reading these craters waterlogged with rain mud blood
I can see a stark hand brandishing nothing through placid
   scum
in a lull of the guns what horror that the livid water
is not shaken by the pity of the tattoo on the dead arm
a heart still held above the despair of the mud
my god the heart on my arm my second birth mark
the rematerialization has picked up these fragments I have
a graft of war and ancient agony forgive
me my dead helper

the sulky pool of mercury stares back at me I am
seeing normally now but I know these flashes will return
from the far past times I gather my wife and son to me
with a fierce gesture that surprises them I am not
a demonstrative man yet how to tell them
what and who I am that we are bound to all that lived
though the barriers are unspeakable we know a little of that
but something what is it gets through it is not
an essence but an energy how it pierces how it
clutches for still as I run my hand through her
amazing hair streaming on my shoulder I feel
a fist shaken in a shell-hole turn in my very marrow
we shall live in the rings of this chain the jeremiahs
who said nothing human would stand are confounded if I
   cry
even the dry tear in my heart that I cannot

stop or if I laugh to think they thought they
could divide the indivisible the old moon's in
the new moon's arms let's take our second
like our first life out from the dome are the suits
ready the mineral storm is quieter it's hard
to go let's go

From the Domain of Arnheim

And so that all these ages, these years
we cast behind us, like the smoke-clouds
dragged back into vacancy when the rocket springs –

The domain of Arnheim was all snow, but we were there.
We saw a yellow light thrown on the icefield
from the huts by the pines, and laughter came up
floating from a white corrie
miles away, clearly.
We moved on down, arm in arm.
I know you would have thought it was a dream,
but we were there. And those were trumpets –
tremendous round the rocks –
while they were burning fires of trash and mammoths'
    bones.
They sang naked, and kissed in the smoke.
A child, or one of their animals, was crying.
Young men blew the ice crystals off their drums.
We came down among them, but of course
they could see nothing, on their time-scale.
Yet they sensed us, stopped, looked up – even into our eyes.
To them we were a displacement of the air,
a sudden chill, yet we had no power
over their fear. If one of them had been dying
he would have died. The crying
came from one just born: that was the cause
of the song. We saw it now. What had we stopped
but joy?
I know you felt
the same dismay, you gripped my arm, they were waiting
for what they knew of us to pass.

A sweating trumpeter took
a brand from the fire with a shout and threw it
where our bodies would have been –
we felt nothing but his courage.
And so they would deal with every imagined power
seen or unseen.
There are no gods in the domain of Arnheim.

We signalled to the ship; got back;
our lives and days returned to us, but
haunted by deeper souvenirs than any rocks or seeds.
From time the souvenirs are deeds.

Floating off to Timor

If only we'd been strangers
we'd be floating off to Timor,
we'd be shimmering on the Trades
in a blue jersey boat
with shandies, flying-fish,
a pace of dolphins
to the copra ports.
And it's no use crying
to me, What dolphins?
for I know where they are
and I'd have snapped you up
and carried you away
snapped you up
and carried you away
if we had been strangers.

But here we are care
of the black roofs.
It's not hard to find
with a collar turned up
and a hoot from the Clyde.
The steps come home
whistling too. And a kettle
steams the cranes out slowly.
It's living with ships
makes a rough springtime
and what heart is safe
when they sing and blow
their music – they seem
to swing at some light rope
like those desires

we keep for strangers.
God, the yellow deck
breathes, and heaves spray
back like a shout!
We're cutting through
some straits of the world
in our old dark room
with salty wings
in the shriek of the dock wind.
But we're caught – meshed
in the fish-scales, ferries,
mudflats and lifebelts
fading into football cries
and the lamps coming on
to bring us in.

We take in
the dream, a cloth from the line
the trains fling sparks on
in our city. We're better awake.
But you know I'd take
you all the same,
if you were my next stranger.

Strawberry Fields Forever

my blackie

                                                        smirr

losing

                                    foxpaw

        patter

                                            your hazel

            whistle

                            dewdrop

        kneedeep

                    unreal

                            the fields we

For Bonfires

1

The leaves are gathered, the trees are dying
for a time.
A seagull cries through white smoke in the garden fires
that fill the heavy air.
All day heavy air
is burning, a moody dog
sniffs and circles the swish of the rake.
In streaks of ash, the gardener drifting
ghostly, beats his hands, a cloud
of breath to the red sun.

2

An island in the city, happy demolition men
behind windowed hoardings — look at them
trailing drills through rubble dust, kicking rubble,
smoking leaning on a pick, putting the stub
over an ear and the hot yellow helmet over that,
whistling up the collapsing chimney, kicking the
ricochet, rattling the trail with
snakes of wire, slamming slabs
down, plaster, cornice, brick, brick
on broken brick and plaster dust,
sprawling with steaming cans and pieces
at noon, afternoon bare sweat shining
paths down chalky backs, coughing
in filtered sunshine, slithering, swearing,
joking, slowly stacking and building
their rubbish into a total bonfire.
Look at that Irishman, bending
in a beautiful arc to throw

the last black rafter to the top,
stands back, walks round it singing
as it crackles into flame – old doors,
old beams, boxes, window-frames,
a rag doll, sacks, flex, old newspapers,
burst shelves, a shoe, old dusters, rags of
wallpaper roses. And they all stand round,
and cheer the tenement to smoke.

3

In a galvanised bucket
the letters burn. They roar and twist
and the leaves curl back one by one.
They put out claws and scrape the iron
like a living thing,
but the scrabbling to be free soon subsides.
The black pages are fused
to a single whispering mass
threaded by dying tracks of gold.
Let them grow cold,
and when they're dead
quickly draw breath.

THE PENGUIN MODERN POETS

All the earlier volumes in this series are still available. The
more recent volumes are:

THE PENGUIN MODERN POETS 6
George MacBeth, Edward Lucie-Smith, and
Jack Clemo

*THE PENGUIN MODERN POETS 7
Richard Murphy, Jon Silkin, and Nathaniel Tarn

*THE PENGUIN MODERN POETS 8
Edwin Brock, Geoffrey Hill, and Stevie Smith

†THE PENGUIN MODERN POETS 9
Denise Levertov, Kenneth Rexroth, and William
Carlos Williams

THE PENGUIN MODERN POETS 10
Adrian Henri, Roger McGough, and Brian Patten

THE PENGUIN MODERN POETS 11
D. M. Black, Peter Redgrove, and D. M. Thomas

*THE PENGUIN MODERN POETS 12
Alan Jackson, Jeff Nuttall, and William Wantling

THE PENGUIN MODERN POETS 13
Charles Bukowski, Philip Lamantia, and
Harold Norse

THE PENGUIN MODERN POETS 14
Alan Brownjohn, Michael Hamburger, and
Charles Tomlinson

*NOT FOR SALE IN THE U.S.A.
†NOT FOR SALE IN THE U.S.A. OR CANADA